PHILOSOPHICAL
RIDINGS

PHILOSOPHICAL RIDINGS

MOTORCYCLES AND THE MEANING OF LIFE

CRAIG BOURNE

ONEWORLD

OXFORD

PHILOSOPHICAL RIDINGS

A Oneworld Book

Published by Oneworld Publications 2007

ISBN-13: 978–1–85168–520–2

Typeset by Jayvee, Trivandrum, India
Cover design by D. R. Ink
Printed and bound by Bell & Bain Ltd., Glasgow

Oneworld Publications
185 Banbury Road
Oxford OX2 7AR
England
www.oneworld-publications.com

Learn more about Oneworld. Join our mailing list to
find out about our latest titles and special offers at:

www.oneworld-publications.com

In memory of Oscar and Benson and all those others who, in their short time, had a good life and died doing what they loved to do.

CONTENTS

ACKNOWLEDGEMENTS

I have discussed some of the topics in this book with the Immoral Sciences Club (the philosophy discussion group I have been running for some of my Cambridge philosophy students). Thanks to those who attended these enjoyable sessions: Bob Beddor, Sarah Boyes, Christina Cameron, Paul Dicken, Sophie Erskine, Claire Fox, Kyla Bowen-la Grange, Chris Korek, Lucy Moseley, Sarah Ramsey, James Sharp and Matt Woodward. Other friends who, for different reasons, deserve a mention are: Josie Cluer, Oren Goldschmidt, David Kelnar, Cait Turvey Roe and Annabelle Ross. Special thanks to Emily Caddick, my pillion in life, mainly for being continually entertaining but at whom I've talked at length about this book without her at any point seeming to lose interest.

I am indebted to St Catharine's College, University of Cambridge for appointing me to a Research Fellowship (2002–2006), which enabled me to write this book between December 2005 and June 2006.

C. P. B.
Cambridge
June 2006

oix

Image 0. Marlon Brando as Johnny, the leader of the Black Rebel Motorcycle Club, in *The Wild One* (1953)

Neutral Gear

Motorcycles and the meaning of life

There is no such thing as the philosophy *of* motorcycles, any more than there is a philosophy of pizza or of haemorrhoids (think about that when you next tuck into your black olives). Motorcycling in itself is just not fundamental enough to the nature of reality or human existence for it to be a philosophical area in its own right in the way that time, space and causation, possibility and necessity, logic and mathematics, thought and language, and right and wrong are. Nevertheless, motorcycles are well-placed (unlike haemorrhoids) to illustrate profound philosophical ideas and the practice of motorcycling raises a host of important philosophical issues, such as the meaning of life and the significance of danger and death, individual freedom and the legitimacy of state interference, our obligations to humans, animals and the environment, and the boundaries of our concept of art. In particular, it raises questions such as: Should I be punished for not wearing a helmet if I don't want to wear one? Is it right to wear leather? Should we be more responsible and use public transport rather than our beloved machines? These are issues that motorcyclists should consider but which are important to everyone. That's why I have written this book. It's for anyone interested in philosophy, or in motor-cycles, or anyone in general who is interested in considering the implications of their lifestyle choices.[1]

This is a book of philosophy, not psychology or sociology or popular culture. What is and what isn't philosophy can per-haps best be illustrated by doing it; by tackling the issues head-on. I won't try to give a watertight definition of philosophy but I hope that anyone who doesn't yet know what it is will have a very good idea by the end of the book. This will also go some way towards answering the question *why* we should do philoso-phy. In approaching the issues in this book from a philosoph-ical viewpoint, we will better appreciate the assumptions on which our beliefs rest and whether those assumptions can be defended. We might find our initial thoughts on a particular issue are wrong and we have to change them, or we might find that they were right and we know that they can be justified. Either way, as a friend of mine once said, we do philosophy because it makes the truth taste even better.

This book is far from the last word on these issues. Each chapter deserves a book-length treatment in its own right. I had

---

[1] Throughout this book I have had to use the term 'motorcycle' rather than 'motorbike' and 'motorcyclist' as a general term for those who ride motorcy-cles, rather than 'biker'. Some British readers may find this use rather stuffy but the reason is that 'motorbike' in some countries, such as the US, refers to mopeds, which is not what I often have in mind. And although 'biker' in the UK is a term for anyone who rides a motorcycle, in some countries it has con-notations of being in a motorcycle gang or being an outlaw motorcyclist. The kind of motorcyclist I mean should be obvious from the context.

to make executive decisions not to develop certain issues further here, make five more invidious distinctions there or be obsessed with subtle matters of interpreting certain texts somewhere else. There is a lot of stuff packed into this book and I thought it best to take certain themes only some way, in order to take others further. However, my primary aim is to provoke further discussion. Although I do put forward particular views, I want people to think for themselves and arrive at their own, well-considered, position on interesting and important matters. I'll be as happy if readers disagree with me as I will if they agree, so long as they have taken the arguments on board and engaged with them properly.

Let us begin, then, by reflecting on the juicy topics of sex, violence and the death wish, before we get on to the more philosophical stuff.

MORBID MOTIVATIONS: THE DEATH WISH

Why do motorcyclists ride? It has been said that only bikers know why dogs stick their heads out of car windows. Anyone who has ever ridden a motorcycle will have a good idea but those on the outside just don't seem to get it. There are a number of theories on why motorcyclists ride, apart from the obvious sensual pleasures of acceleration and so on, and the subtle pleasure of manipulating an instrument skilfully. However, as some outside motorcycling have suspected, there may be darker impulses at play under the surface.

According to the influential work of Sigmund Freud (1856–1939), the so-called father of psychoanalysis, two basic instincts interact in various ways to drive humans and account for their mental lives: the *sex drive* (what he calls 'Eros') and the *death instinct* (more commonly known as the 'death wish'). The sex drive binds people together, whereas the death instinct is destructive in nature (Freud 1938: 148). The underlying mechanism for both is the so-called 'Nirvana principle', according to which organisms aim to reach a state of tranquillity by discharging their tensions; for example, after a build-up of sexual urges, the sexual act culminates in a feeling of balance, completeness and satisfaction. The goal, according to Freud, is the final tranquil state. By extension, since the ultimate state of tranquillity is being in the state of death, that's one of our goals; that's why we seek it, each in our own way, such as on a motorcycle. We shall see in the next chapter, on death, that this is completely misguided, since death is not a state of emotional equilibrium, at least in any non-trivial sense. Nevertheless, Freud writes: 'It seems, then, that an instinct is an urge inherent in organic life to restore an earlier stage of things which the living entity has been obliged to abandon under the pressure of external disturbing forces' (Freud 1920: 36).

Since organic things (those things made from carbon, such as humans) arrived much later in the history of the world than the inorganic, the earlier stage of things to be restored to which Freud alludes must be the state before life:

> If we are to take it as a truth that knows no exception that everything living dies for internal reasons – become inorganic once again – then we shall be compelled to say that 'the aim of all life is death' and, looking backwards, that 'inanimate things existed before living ones'.

> (Freud 1920: 38)

We now know, then, what people are asking when they ask us whether we have a death wish, which they often do when they find out we ride a motorcycle. Since Freud meant his theory to apply to everyone – not just thrill seekers – the correct response should be that, if anyone has a death wish, we all do (although it might be more obvious in the case of thrill seekers than others). For many, me included, this will sound too far-fetched a theory but since it is supposed to apply to everyone, it doesn't explain what we thought it might anyway. If everyone has a death wish, this doesn't by itself explain why some choose motorcycles rather than another pursuit, unless the theory does *not* apply to everyone, in which case there might be a special breed of people who do have a death wish, motorcyclists included. Maybe. However, this is not for the philosopher to resolve but a matter for psychoanalysts and the good judgement of the reader.

A way in which this issue might be of further interest to motorcyclists is in how it might relate to the more well-known images associated with the biker. According to Freud, aggression arises from the death instinct being turned outwards towards the world. This, Freud thinks, has serious implications for the future of civilisation. He writes:

[Civilisation is] a process in the service of Eros [that is, the sex drive], whose purpose is to combine single human individuals and after that families, then races, peoples and nations, into one great unity, the unity of mankind. But man's natural aggressive instinct, the hostility of each against all and all against each, oppose this programme of civilisation. This aggressive instinct is the derivative and the main representative of the death instinct which we have found alongside Eros and which shares world-dominion with it. And now, I think, the meaning of the evolution of civilisation is no longer obscure to us. It must present the struggle between Eros and Death, between the instinct of life and the instinct of destruction as it works itself out in the human species. This struggle is what all life essentially consists of and the evolution of civilisation may therefore be simply described as the struggle for life of the human species. And it is this battle of the giants that our nursemaids try to appease with their lullaby about Heaven.

(Freud 1930: 122)

Let us investigate the close link between the traditional biker image and sex and aggression.

LEATHER, SEX AND VIOLENCE: A DAY IN THE LIFE OF A BIKER?

It seems to be a plausible hypothesis that the traditional biker image of the leather-clad rebel arose from certain films of the 1950s, in particular László Benedek's *The Wild One* (1953), which was based on the real-life riots that took place during a three-day biker convention in Hollister, California in July 1947. The adoption of leather as the hero's garb is explained by its associations with military uniforms: many of the motorcycle clubs of the 1940s and 1950s were formed by GIs returning from World War II; leather jackets were part of their kit. However, it is perhaps the links with the German aviators of World War I, who wore black leather jackets and its later wear by the Nazis of World War II that best explains leather's association with aggression.[2]

Where does the association of motorcycles and sex come from? Although it is less usual for motorcycles to become fetish objects, it is rather common for leather to be fetishised; given the association between power, danger and leather, this is one plausible link between motorcycles and sex. (Is there any other reason why Kenneth Anger's film *Scorpio Rising* (1964) features an army of gay Nazi bikers?) Are there other ways to link sex and the motorcycle? What about the obvious physiological effects of the vibrations of a throbbing engine between the legs? This partly accounts for it, no doubt, but it's not the whole story. Is it that Marlon Brando, who played the hero Johnny in *The Wild One* (see Image 0), is generally considered to be rather attractive and so motorcycles have, by association, soaked into the collective consciousness as steeped in sexuality (particularly as Brando portrayed a sexual predator)? Perhaps, but it's not entirely convincing: many people haven't even seen *The Wild One*, yet associate biking and bikers with sexuality and danger. Nevertheless, a plausible story can be told.

The Wild One caught people's imagination; real-life bikers wanted to associate themselves with this powerful image and later films (with attractive actors) reflected what real-life bikers were doing, reinforcing the image real-life bikers wanted to have and so on, round the cycle. Most of us have inherited this image, lying at the end of a chain of films related to its

[2] See Ferriss (2006) for a nice, fuller account of the link between sex and biker style. See also Polhemus (2001) and Simon (2001) for a development of some of the themes of this section.

original sources; it doesn't matter that we weren't there from the start. Indeed, *The Wild One* influenced subsequent films, not only in the characters that were portrayed but in the techniques that were used to portray them. The opening shot of *The Wild One*, for instance, is taken as if the viewer were lying in the middle of an open road looking towards the horizon. It becomes apparent that the dots in the distance are motorcycles racing towards the camera, which eventually race past and almost crash into the lens. As Simon (2001) points out, this technique was used in subsequent films, and for a very good reason: the camera angle and framing set up a perspective that makes us vulnerable to the motorcycles that endanger anything in their path. Not only this, the shot emphasises the road in the biker's identity, making him more threatening because it symbolises his mobility, which translates to his lack of any real home or obligations and commitments to anyone or anything. He's a stranger. Such a lack of commitment was associated both with sexual promiscuity and a disrespect for people and their property. The motorcycle's association with sex and aggression, power and danger – both of the motorcycling itself and the one who rides – is a complex mixture of these factors.

Perhaps it was this that made more palatable a rather strange attempt of some psychiatrists to classify the desire to ride a motorcycle as a mental illness. In an article in *Time* magazine, a Harvard Medical School psychiatrist claimed that enthusiasm for motorcycle riding was 'a hitherto unrecognised emotional ailment' and that he 'found the same basic symptoms in all his sick cyclists', such as promiscuity, impotency and being 'always worried about discovering that they were homosexuals'.[3] Furthermore, riders 'used their motorcycles to compensate for feelings of effeminacy and weakness'. Such theories were actually taken seriously and published in the *American Journal of Psychiatry*.[4] Yet, even though we can find the theory lacking as a general theory about all bikers, it is understandable against the background iconic image of the biker: if being a biker is about machismo, toughness, virility and independence, it may well be that some don the clothing and straddle the motorcycle to make up for their perceived inadequacies.

It is interesting to note a twist in this tale; at the time of its release, a significant number of viewers of *The Wild One* complained that Marlon Brando was too effeminate in his leather jacket and cap; he wasn't considered masculine at all and many bikers of the time didn't relate to his character. However, due to the influence of the film, this image soon became *the* image bikers adopted, and which became associated with an expression of heterosexual masculinity. It must be said that the image is now considered to be one of the classic homosexual looks but either way, it is a highly sexualised look. I think the case has been made. Those still not convinced about the link between sex, aggression and the motorcycle should explain Halle Berry's appearance in *Catwoman* (2004) on a Ducati Monster and wearing some quite amazing tight black leather outfits, Alicia Silverstone's appearance as leather-clad biker Batgirl in *Batman and Robin* (1997) and why the 'bad-and-sadistic' girl in *Torque* (2004) is dressed in equally eye-catching black leather, while the 'good-not-sadistic-yet-still-feisty-and-with-an-edge'

---

[3] 'The Motorcycle Syndrome', *Time* (7 December 1970)
[4] The source of this brilliant tale is Kieffner (2006: 169)

girl dresses in blue and white leathers. (Discerning cinemagoers will also have noted the strong correlation between sex, aggression, the motorcycle and truly appalling films. However, Uma Thurman's appearance in the coolest, Bruce-Lee-esque, yellow leathers with black stripe, in the astonishing *Kill Bill: Vol.1* (2003) is a notable exception (see Image 4).)

It isn't my job as a philosopher to comment on any of these sexy and sadistic issues but, nevertheless, *The Wild One* introduces us to an influential philosophical problem. In portraying the biker as a stranger with no commitments to anyone or anything, the film encapsulates the central thrust of the philosophical idea of nihilism.

THE WILL TO (HORSE) POWER

Nihilism is, perhaps, most famously associated with the German philosopher Friedrich Nietzsche (1844–1900). According to Nietzsche, humans have lost their belief in God (by which he means any kind of external standard or absolute being against which to measure this-worldly existence); they have lost the basis for their values. All kinds of standards set by morality, rationality and the truth no longer have anything to ground them; no more can an appeal be made to an absolute standard; neither God, The Good nor The Truth can any longer tell us what is right and what is wrong. This, for Nietzsche, is a rather dangerous situation for humans to find themselves in. In his book *The Will to Power*, Nietzsche calls nihilism 'the danger of dangers', for one reaction to the realisation that traditional values have no firm basis is to reject the notion entirely, to believe that ultimately nothing is worthwhile and to think that forging relationships with others and making commitments to projects is pointless. We are left with only one purpose: to destroy.

It isn't entirely clear why this wretched existence should result from the loss of a belief in God or any other absolute standard. It is especially unclear why *destruction* should follow from having no values, rather than it resulting in a bland world of harmless, lethargic, apathetic depressives. Maybe it is just a fact that humans – at least some humans – if they have no purpose, go on the rampage. It may even be that Freud supplies the psychoanalytic underpinning for nihilism. Maybe it is because the balance between Eros and the death instinct has been shifted: the positive Eros, which represents value, has been undermined and the death instinct has taken over. Perhaps. It is undoubtedly true that, as a matter of fact, people do associate a nasty and brutish existence with the abandonment of so-called 'traditional' values, and it is this that is reflected in the biker cultures that have emerged since the 1950s.

Consider the course 'Dangerous Motorcycle Gangs' given by certain American police forces; a beautiful illustration of how much of an outsider and transgressor of all that is moral the biker is perceived to be. The course warns that a white cross on a biker's colours means that the wearer has robbed a grave, a red cross that they have performed homosexual fellatio with witnesses present, green wings that they have performed cunnilingus on a woman with venereal disease, and purple wings that the woman on whom the cunnilingus was performed was dead (see Pratt 2006: 82). Well, I'd have hated to have been at that party; but I suspect this tale more illustrates the dangers of taking certain people to be 'other'; reflecting the susceptibility of some to believe all sorts of nonsense about people who do not fit in with what they perceive as normal. This is dangerous in many different ways, since it feeds our fears of things we don't quite understand. It forms the basis of racism, homophobia or of waging war on others with a clear conscience, because we don't need to justify how we treat those we take to be alien. I'm not so sure that the bikers themselves, for a bit of a laugh, didn't perpetuate stories about the symbols on their jackets that the gullible authorities swallowed. (Even if such activities did take place, it's hard to imagine they would be widespread.) It seems best to treat this myth as harmless fun but when the myths are circulated about a particular class of people, such as in governmental war propaganda, or by the media, this can endanger solutions to serious problems; they are more likely to whip people up into an irrational frenzy, which does nobody any good.

This issue takes us too far away from our main theme, so I shall say no more. However, it is worth pointing out that it shows we should be wary of classifying people, not only for the clichéd reasons that will be all too familiar to anyone who watches daytime television talk shows but also because in identifying ourselves with a particular kind of person, we run the risk of leading an *inauthentic* lifestyle.

The French novelist and philosopher Jean-Paul Sartre (1905–1980) captured this with his characteristically insightful observations, some of which centre on people who *act a part*. His famous example is of the waiter who 'plays at *being* a waiter in a café' (Sartre 1958: 59) – an example that, ironically, has introduced to the popular imagination the idea that to play the rôle of the French intellectual, one must frequent cafés; but anyway ...[5] The waiter is well-chosen; we often see these overly camp men fawning over customers, almost dancing round tables while carrying trays of drinks. The waiter does this because, he thinks, *that's what waiters do*. Again, somewhat ironically, those associated with the theatre – luvvies – can be spotted a mile off (in the UK at least) even when they are not officially supposed to be acting, since they typically flounce around in their chiffon scarves and 'ethnic' skirts, calling everyone 'darling' and kissing those around them on the cheeks (on the face, that is). This playing is also apparent in less overt cases. No doubt we are all prone to melodramatic episodes, by which I don't only mean swooning at every opportunity but overindulging ourselves in a particular moment. Our reasons will be many and varied and there is perhaps nothing harmful in it, in itself. However, when people identify themselves with a particular kind of person and then try to excuse their behaviour by saying that that is just what people of this kind do, they are living inauthentically. We all know people who play the rôle of the victim, who define themselves in terms of a bad thing that has happened to them and may try to excuse or explain other things they do in terms of that; but this is to refuse to live up to what we really are: free beings who can choose what we want to be. It's tempting to describe other cases where this playing occurs but since we are interested in motorcycles, let's consider how this pans out in the case of the biker and bring it back to what provoked this discussion; nihilism.

---

[5] The person who impersonates himself also occurs in Sartre's novels, such as the barman in *The Age of Reason* who is 'impersonating a barman' (1945a: 173) and Daniel in *The Reprieve*: 'he who sees me causes me to be: I am as he sees me' (1945b: 345).

The French-Algerian novelist Albert Camus (1913–1960) asserted that people have two choices in the face of the ground-lessness of our values: to commit suicide or to rebel. Perhaps, if we follow Freud, we are all really trying to commit suicide; but it is the theme of rebellion that is taken up in *The Wild One* and subsequent American films such as Francis Ford Coppola's *Rumblefish* (1983). To a certain extent, such a portrayal of rebellion and the rejection of traditional values seems to reflect and be reflected by real-life biker lifestyles. (Or, at least, to reflect the image of the biker that some bikers like to portray, which is what lies behind the 'Dangerous Motorcycle Gangs' course.) There is no doubt that civil unrest has been caused by certain motorcycle gangs. And not just in America. The Japanese have *bosozoku* (see Sato 2001) and from the late 1950s to the mid-1960s, the UK saw clashes between the well-dressed Lambretta and Vespa scooter-riding 'Mods' and the leather-clad 'Rocker' biker gangs. These clashes are thought to be one of the inspirations for Anthony Burgess's magnificent 1962 novel *A Clockwork Orange* and when the 1979 film *Quadrophenia* (based on the 1973 album by *The Who*) cele-brated the Mod movement and glamorised the real-life fighting which took place on Brighton beach between the Mods and the Rockers, a revival of the movement occurred.

But at what is such a rebellion directed? The universe? Other people? What is its reason? What could it achieve? How is it an answer to the problem with which nihilism leaves us? Johnny, in *The Wild One*, has evidently adopted such a half-baked, vague notion of rebellion. When Johnny and Chico (Lee Marvin) fight and someone asks what the fight is about, the elderly coffee shop owner astutely comments, 'Dunno. [They] don't know themselves, probably'. And when asked, 'What are you rebelling against, Johnny?' he replies, 'Waddaya got?' He evidently wants to give the impression that he is clear about what he is rebelling against: everything. But he's not at all clear. He can't give a straight answer because he has no straight answer to give. Somewhere along the line, the real message of the film has been lost and Johnny and his kind have been hailed as heroes to be emulated rather than as fools to be ridiculed. His real standing is summed up by the Sheriff's admonishment: 'I don't get you. I don't get your act at all. And I don't think you do either. I don't think you know what you're trying to do or how to go about it. I think you're stupid, real stupid.'

How did this character become such an icon? Can the same be asked of all the other bores who turn up in similar films, acting cool but having nothing interesting to say for themselves, such as Motorcycle Boy (Mickey Rourke) in *Rumblefish*? The truth is that they are nothing but pathetic charlatans who fumble around with no direction, surrounded by mindless morons who blindly follow them. This is living inauthentically in its purest form. They are *playing* at being rebels, as much as the waiter is playing at being a waiter. It is no solution to nihilism to join a gang, destroy things for the sake of it and jump around on pogo sticks – how very rock 'n' roll! – as some do in *The Wild One*.[6] Rebellion *with* a cause can deserve our

---

[6] Note how different these characters are from Alex in *A Clockwork Orange*, whose destructive tendencies seem to be driven by an aesthetic vision – he certainly does have a brutal authenticity about him. As for the others, maybe times have moved on. *The Wild One* looks rather feeble to modern cinemagoers. If you want to see a good film, I wouldn't watch it, unless you fancy a good laugh at the special effects and awful dialogue (although Johnny's Triumph Thunderbird 6T and the other bikes are nice to look at). The same

admiration but rebellion *without* one deserves our contempt –
it doesn't even count as rebellion; it's just confusion.

We won't learn anything philosophically interesting, then,
in considering Johnny's lifestyle. But we don't need to.
Reflecting on our own riding experiences gives us immediate
access to some of the more profound and influential insights
offered by the so-called 'existentialists' in response to nihilism.
Let us start with the notion of angst.

ANGST, AUTHENTICITY, FREEDOM AND MEANINGFULNESS

You're riding at high speed in the fast lane of the motorway. On
one side is the central reservation.[7] Just a little nudge of the
handlebars or a lean to the side and you'd go crashing into the
barrier. You know this and the thought is exquisite. Of course,
you don't do it. But at this point you become starkly aware of
the possibilities; primarily, the possibility of your own death.
This is existential angst.

'Angst' has rather dark and depressing connotations in the
English language, often associated with problematic teenagers

goes for the more recent *Rumblefish*, only there's no nice bike and nothing to
laugh about, unless mind-numbing boredom tickles you. This uninteresting
kind of rebellion is represented in even more recent films such as *Torque*,
which is equally unappealing. *Biker Boyz* (2003) has its cringe-worthy and
silly moments, although the stunts, to a certain extent, make up for them. One
lesson to be learned is that rebel biker films hardly ever work. This isn't to say
I wouldn't welcome more bike scenes in your average action film; these are
often the only good things about some of them. Think of the Triumph Speed
Triple duel at the end of the otherwise dreadful *Mission: Impossible II* (2000).
Nevertheless, the occasional great film based on or enhanced by, motorcycles
is sometimes released and I have cited some in this book.

[7] That is, the part of the motorway that protects you from oncoming
traffic. I believe this is known as the 'median' in the US.

in black T-shirts and dark nail polish but it need not be like this, as we can see from the feelings of exhilaration and liberation you get from situations like that just described. Motorcyclists, more than anyone else on the road, are continually reminded of their mortality. And through the notion of angst, we can put some flesh on the rather vague association of freedom with motorcycling. This is a quite different kind of freedom from political freedom (or 'liberty'), which I discuss later, in the chapter on speeding and the legitimacy of helmet laws. The kind of freedom we are talking about, as embodied in feelings of angst, can be called 'existential freedom'.

According to Sartre, this profound sense of freedom, generated by reflecting on all of the possibilities that are open to us – we could choose to do *any* of them – means we find it hard to justify what grounds there are for choosing one rather than another.[8] None is on firmer foundations than the others. The firm foundation of our own essential nature, which we thought we could rely on to take us in one direction rather than another, giving us a sense of security and protecting us from having to take responsibility for our lives, starts to show itself as an illusion. At this point, awareness of their complete freedom to realise their potential leads some to feel 'anguish'. They don't like it and so they pretend that they are not as free as they are. Sartre says that these people act in 'bad faith', which amounts to the same thing as the inauthentic lifestyle mentioned

---

[8] Within reason, of course. We couldn't decide to fly or win the lottery or choose to eat gravel rather than food. For Sartre, our freedom is always set against a background of 'facticity': we are constrained by our physical situation but we still have much more freedom within these constraints than many people realise.

above. People identify themselves with a type of person and so claim not to be able to do other than what that sort of person does. This gives them a security blanket but in doing it, they deny their freedom.

What else are we meant to do, in the light of such freedom and the apparent groundlessness of our values? Should we simply acknowledge the meaningless of our existence and hang around until our miserable deaths? This is no solution; it is giving up. Suicide is better – at least it gives you control over your own death and allows you to leave with dignity. Rebellion is another option. Yet, as we saw with *The Wild One*, mere undirected rebellion does not salvage any notion of meaning, so that is no solution either. But we have to be careful with the term 'rebel'. Although it conjures up all sorts of biker images, there are different ways in which we can rebel. Camus would not suggest that we rebel by joining Johnny's Black Rebel Motorcycle Club but rather that we should rebel by sticking our middle finger up at the cold and indifferent universe and *living our lives to the full regardless*. Sartre, like Nietzsche before him, proposes that we take life by the scruff of the neck and *create* meanings for our lives. Sartre prescribes doing this through acts of freedom. In this way, we live an authentic life by using our freedom to create meaning for it (and in the process we create ourselves: we *are* what we *do*). Be creative; original; daring. Stand up for what you believe in and value, even if, ultimately, it has no firmer foundations than those laid by humans themselves. This is a much better approach.

And it is an approach that fits best with the great films in which motorcycles feature. Virgil Hilt's (Steve McQueen's) heroic attempt to break to freedom on a Triumph TT Special 650 in

The Great Escape (1963) is deservedly iconic.[9] The story of Burt Munro's perseverance in breaking motorcycle speed records, as portrayed by Anthony Hopkins in *The World's Fastest Indian* (2005), is truly life-affirming (see Image 3). Ewan McGregor's 19,000-mile trip around the world with Charley Boorman, on BMW 1150GS bikes, documented in *Long Way Round* (2004), epitomises the virtues of spirit and endurance, as, to a certain extent, does Che Guevara's road trip around South America on a 1939 Norton 500cc single, depicted in *The Motorcycle Diaries* (2004) (although, it must be said, he only managed part of the journey on it and whether we would want to be as positive about the rest of his life and legacy is not at all clear). In the film *Heartlands* (2002), which is relatively unknown but deserves more attention, a darts fanatic, Colin, travels across the Peak District from the Midlands to the northwest of England to save his marriage, while having his life transformed along the way – and all on a Honda 50 (see Image 5)! The Harley enthusiast Rocky Dennis, afflicted with craniodiaphyseal dysplasia ('lionitis' – an extremely rare, disfiguring, sclerotic bone disorder) on whom the film *Mask* (1985) was based, is an inspiration to those who think they have it bad. All these films, in their different ways – from grand and spectacular feats to more commonplace displays of compassion and humour – express an effective and dignified vision of human integrity and authenticity; a proper response to nihilism that far outstrips the crude and rather ridiculous 'rebellious' response of Johnny in *The Wild One*.

---

[9] I don't just mean to use this to illustrate the obvious sense in which this is rebellious, namely as against a wicked oppressor (which already makes it far superior to Johnny's rebellion). It is also rebellious in that it shows that some values, like freedom, are worth fighting for, despite the universe not caring.

Can we live with this dual picture of the meaningfulness of our lives? Life, as observed from the outside – the 'god's eye' perspective – doesn't amount to a hill of beans: in the whole scheme of things, we are insignificant specs. However, viewing life as lived from the inside – the 'dog's eye' perspective – it is infused with meaning and value. What should our attitude be towards these two thoughts? The tension between them is known as the 'paradox of the absurd': how can we reconcile the fact that we take life seriously with the fact that, in the whole scheme of things, we don't think it has any significant value? Is it absurd to put so much effort into something you think is ultimately pointless?

Many have simply embraced this absurdity; but we have only *assumed*, so far, that our lives are, in the whole scheme of things, meaningless, from which it follows that the way we carry on is absurd. What are the grounds for thinking it meaningless? When considering angst, we noted that we were free to crash into the central reservation; death was one of the possibilities; but death is inevitable whatever we do. It is this that many think is the root of the ultimate futility of all of our actions; it is not uncommon for people to think, 'What's the point if we are all going to die?'

But would immortality help make our lives any more meaningful? The British philosopher Bernard Williams (1929–2003) put the issue as follows: for an immortal life to be meaningful, it would have to be attractive for the person whose life it would be (see Williams 1973). To remain the same person over time, Williams claims, we must retain the same kinds of interests, dispositions and goals. Were we to have the same interests, dispositions and goals over an immortal lifetime, our lives would be endlessly boring. Yet, if we tried to change these basic ingredients of who we are, life would be varied and not at all boring but this would come at the cost of not being able to say it was the *same* person throughout the duration of the life. Williams concludes that immortal life is either unattractive for a single person or attractive but not the life of a single person. So immortality would not make *our* lives meaningful.

The first thing to question is why such a life would give rise to such tedium. We often get engrossed in an activity, get bored, do something else interesting, get bored, go back to something we haven't done for a while when we are interested in pursuing it again and so on. We can do all of this without feeling that we have in any way changed who we are. If someone lives a mortal life in this way, it is not clear why they would not be just as ful-filled living an immortal life in the same way. The second thing to question is whether, in changing our characters, we become a different person. So long as the change is a gradual one, such that we can see that there is the right sort of link between one stage of our life and another, even though the person of 2010 does not much resemble the person of 2110, we may well want to say that it is the same person.[10] It is not clear that we would be as indifferent to that person as we would be to anyone else in 2110, since we may well still feel a certain amount of pride (or disappointment) in their achievements. Williams' arguments against thinking of an immortal life as an attractive one are not very compelling.

We should not conclude from this that immortality would make our lives more meaningful than mortality, for how would it help to clarify the point of our lives if we supposed we were immortal? Immortality might allow you to do more things but

[10] See Lewis (1976) for an account of what to say about personal identity over long durations.

if you don't think that the things you can do during a mortal lifetime are meaningful in themselves, it is hard to see how adding an infinite amount of those things together can amount to a meaningful life. Adding nothing to nothing, no matter how many times you do it, results in more nothing. Whether we die or not cannot be the real issue.

This is not an argument for thinking that life is, therefore, meaningless whether we are immortal or not. Rather, I take it to be an argument for casting *doubt* on the application of the notion of meaninglessness to life itself. Even to understand the question of whether life is meaningful or not we would have to be given conditions under which it would *count* as being meaningful and conditions under which it would count as being meaningless. Unless we are given those conditions, we do not know how to answer the question; the question would be of doubtful coherence. Immortality was offered as a condition for life being meaningful but this failed. If we cannot propose any other conditions under which we would count life as meaning*ful*, we cannot have a clear grasp of what it means for life to be meaning*less*. So, although, at first sight, it looked perfectly legitimate to formulate a judgement concerning the meaningfulness of life from the god's eye perspective, on further reflection, it isn't.

Consider how different this situation is from the dog's eye perspective. We can state conditions under which our activities are pointless and contrast them with conditions under which they aren't. What would we think of someone who thought the best way to become a great musician was regularly to slam a car door on his fingers? We'd think it was pointless; the right means to achieve the goal are not being used and the strategy is positively damaging any chance of success. What about someone going to the gym every morning to build up their arms so that eventually they'd be able to flap quickly enough to fly? That's pointless, because it is physically impossible. What about buying a load of high-tech MotoGP kit for our motorcycles? This would be pointless because we'd never be in a position to take full advantage of it. What about applying for the top job in a company when we have only worked there for a few weeks? This is pointless because we're not up to it and nobody would think we were. What about spending your days like the mythical Sisyphus, who, after upsetting the gods, was condemned to an eternal cycle of pushing a boulder up a large hill and watching it roll down again? This is pointless because there is no payoff at the end. (We can imagine variations on this theme: Sisyphus on a game show or enjoying what he is doing or where there are intricate rules, techniques and styles such that connoisseurs could judge good push from poor. Under these circumstances, it may well be a meaningful activity but by our current standards of evaluation, it is pointless.) There are many and varied ways in which an activity can be said to have a point and make life meaningful, and we have no difficulty at all in specifying in what ways it has or does not have one. However, the same simply cannot be said for making judgements from the god's eye perspective about the meaningfulness of life.

This discussion started with nihilism and there being no god (or other absolute standards) in our lives. But let us suppose that God does exist and plays an active part. Is this the required condition for us to have meaningful lives? It is difficult to see how. Some claim to have a purpose in their lives because they have chosen to devote their lives to God, but this pushes back the question of the point of *his* existence. Perhaps he doesn't need a point; he is an end in himself. But if so, how is this any different to someone who feels they have a purpose in their lives because they devote their lives to playing the guitar? What more are we asking for, when we ask about the meaning of our lives, over and above what can be said when we are engaged in pursuits that we take to be of value? Someone might ask why we are engaged in a certain activity. They might ask why we are cleaning our motorcycle and when we explain about corrosion, might then ask why we would want to stop it from corroding; when we explain about wanting a functioning bike, they might ask why we want to continue riding on a functioning bike, at which point we explain that the whole experience is ultimately something we value but that we cannot give any more explanation. But to say that there is no *further* justification for something does not mean that there is *no* reason to do it. If someone asks you why you don't want to do something and you reply that it is because it is painful, there is not much more you can say when they ask why that should stop you from doing it. Nobody would take this inability to give a *further* justification to mean that there is *no* good reason for not doing it. Some things need no further justification. That's the basis for the difference between something that is of *instrumental* value and something that is of *intrinsic* value and not for the difference between something that has value and something that hasn't.[11]

---

[11] That is, this is the difference between something not valued in itself but valuable because it facilitates doing other things of value (instrumentally valuable) and something valuable in its own right (intrinsically valuable). See the chapter on our obligations to the environment for more on this distinction.

In short, we have no good grounds for thinking that our lives are meaningless from the god's eye perspective because we do not know what conditions would have to be in place before we were willing to say it was meaningful. Since our lives, from the dog's eye perspective, can be perfectly meaningful, those lives, even though they be packed with absurdities, cannot in themselves be said to be absurd. Because we have the ability to recognise these situations and employ the term correctly from the dog's eye view, we should not be conned into thinking that we can go further and apply it from the god's eye view. Our attitude need neither be one of despair, of the existentialist's contempt nor of irony (as Nagel 1971 suggests). Our attitude, if our lives are going well relative to the standards we have in place, should be of unproblematic contentment. What we shouldn't do, even if someone does make sense of the idea that life itself is meaningless, is follow Johnny down his road. What we should rather try to do is catch up with the likes of Burt Munro.

We have seen the extent to which death gives meaning to life – that is, not much – but we should discuss further the nature of death, since, as riders of dangerous machines, it is an issue we have all thought about and need to have a clear idea of.

Image 1. Death personified and her biker aides in Jean Cocteau's *Orphée* (1950)

First Gear

The end of the road: what's so bad about death?

Tom: Aren't you scared you'll kill yourself, if you crash?
Burt Munro: No. You live more in five minutes on a bike
like this going flat out than some people live in a lifetime.

The World's Fastest Indian (2005)

Riding a bike, whether on the race track or the road, is, like many life-enhancing activities, a dangerous pursuit – think of the Isle of Man TT motorcycle festival! For many, the risks involved constitute part of the thrill of riding and form the basis of the familiar romanticised image of the biker. Death is a familiar topic of conversation for anyone associated with bikes, since, all too commonly, motorcycle accidents result in fatalities. The latest UK government figures, at the time of writing, show that 693 motorcyclists were killed in road accidents in 2003 and 6959 were seriously injured. Motorcyclists represent only one per cent of all traffic, yet twenty per cent of deaths and serious injuries; motorcycle riders are statistically forty times more likely to be killed than car drivers. Motorcyclists *should* take the topic of death seriously.

In many cases – but certainly not all – it is natural and appropriate to count the loss of life as tragic. Why? This may strike some as an odd question. We are frequently told that we must be mad to ride a motorcycle, because one day we'll kill ourselves; for some, this is a good enough reason not to ride. However, for someone who questions why that should be any reason to stop riding, a bare assertion that death is bad, without any argument, leaves it without force. We need first to clarify a host of philosophical questions about death before we even begin to take it into consideration when making a decision about what to do with our lives. We need to ask the whos, whats, whys and whens of death. We need to know *what* death is, *why* it should be taken to be a harm, *when* the harm, if it is a harm, is supposed to occur and to *whom* it is supposed to be a harm. These are not straightforward questions.

WHAT IS DEATH?

Many people have heard that two definitions of death count for medical and legal purposes. One defines death in terms of the non-functioning of the brain (sometimes called 'brain death'), the other defines it in terms of the non-functioning of the heart and lungs (sometimes called 'clinical death'). However, for our purposes, it is not good enough simply to give a medical definition of what death is because to say that death occurs when the brain or heart and lungs stop functioning does not *explain* what it is about those states of the body that gives rise to our treating the person differently. Such a change in our physiological state does not in itself give us any reason for thinking that such an event is either a tragedy or a relief. Neither does it give us any reason for taking a person's organs to benefit others, for allowing their spouse to remarry without a divorce, for burying the person in the ground or burning them in a furnace, or for dividing their possessions among family and friends. These things would be outrageous, if done to a living person. What is it about these medical definitions of death which allows such acts to take place? What is it about the state of the body following brain death, but not its state after an appendectomy, that explains why we can legitimately do such things?

Such medical criteria for death can plausibly only be considered to be *tests* for the state we call 'death', rather than as *constituting* death. This is why the heart-lung definition of death is hardly ever used now; medical advances have allowed people to be kept in a state that we would clearly count as being alive, under conditions of heart-lung death. The heart-lung definition gives rise to the dramatic tales of those who claim that they were technically dead in the operating theatre and had to be brought back to life. Before certain advances in medicine, the heart-lung definition was a good one, since heart-lung failure meant something significant for the proper functioning of a person, which didn't allow them to go on living. In the same way, it may well be that, in the future, the non-functioning of a specific biological brain will no longer serve as a sufficient condition for saying that the person has died. Cloned brains or computer technology could well be developed that would keep the person alive and brain death would not constitute the death of the person.

It seems we should view these medical tests for death as showing, at a given point in time, what sort of biological support would be required for a person to go on living: these functions *facilitate* living but don't *constitute* it. This raises the question of what is living. It strikes me that this is not a *factual* question that can be settled by science but an *ethical* question, in that it concerns what sorts of things we value. We may be able to maintain the vital organs in a body by mechanical means but when other aspects, which we think are important to that body having a life, are lacking, such as a certain amount of autonomy or consciousness, we are disinclined to call that body 'living'. Living, for human beings, is enjoying the pleasure of making someone laugh, being left breathless by a sublime piece of music, feeling touched by a subtle gesture, being amused by the seriousness of small children, engaging in intellectual pursuits and artistic creation, contributing to making the world a worthwhile place in which to live, or experiencing the sense of fear and dread when negotiating a steep, winding, mountain road in torrential rain with just first gear, a couple of trusty brakes and your nerve to keep you from falling over the edge.[1]

We have, I take it, a fairly robust idea of what it is to have a life. There may be difficult cases, such as those in persistent

---

[1] This happened to me when I went to stay with some friends in the breathtaking Lake District in Cumbria, England, riding via the Hardknott Pass towards Wastwater, from Ambleside. Not only was I not told about the narrow roads with sheer drops along the edges, I was also not told that, with an overall gradient of 1 in 3 (33 per cent) and up to 1 in 2.5 in places, Hardknott Pass is the steepest road in England! The moral is that motorcyclists without a death wish should be wary of the advice they receive from non-motorcyclist friends concerning 'pleasant' routes!

vegetative states, who, although unconscious, display certain behaviour, such as response to pain, opening their eyes, smiling, crying but not much else.[2] Our concept of what it is to have a life may not be robust enough to determine what to say in these cases, which is more evidence to suggest that it is more a matter to be settled by what we value than a matter of which science can discover the answer. Whichever way we decide, it is clear that death is whatever life isn't. We know that much about death but is it the sort of thing which should be considered to be a harm?

IS DEATH A HARM?

There is a difference between *dying* and *death*. Dying is a legitimate part of living; death isn't. As the Austrian philosopher Ludwig Wittgenstein (1889–1951) said, 'Death is not an event of life. Death is not lived through' (Wittgenstein 1921: §6.4311). Although we all are, in a sense, dying, we often only use the term to signify a bodily process, such as due to illness or organ failure, which, given the current state of medical science, culminates in a death that is either premature or predictable. This may not cover everything but it covers the clear-cut cases, such as dying from old age or cancer or the short period between a road accident and death. We know that dying can be a long and painful process for the one dying as well as for their friends and family. Dying, despite any benefits it might give rise to, such as the bringing together of a family or the spurring on of the dying

[2] I will not discuss further the ethical and legal problems raised by these medical cases. For a very readable and thought-provoking treatment of the issues, see Singer (1995).

person to do great things, can certainly be considered to be a harm to the one dying.

It is not clear that the same reasons can brought for thinking that *death* can be a harm (or a benefit) to the one who dies. We certainly think that the premature death of a loved one is a tragedy and the death of someone in chronic pain a relief. However, although *we* certainly feel the harm or the benefit of the death of a person, the person themselves cannot appreciate anything – they are, after all, dead. They feel no pain; they feel no relief; they feel nothing. In what sense can death be a harm or a benefit to the one who dies?

The Ancient Greek philosopher Epicurus (341–270 BCE), whose essential claim was that a proper understanding of how the world works would rid humans of superficial cares and needless feelings of anxiety, superstition and fear, took these considerations to show that death is something that cannot be considered a harm. He famously wrote, in *Letter to Menoeceus*:

> So death, the most terrifying of ills, is nothing to us, since so long as we exist, death is not with us; but when death comes, then we do not exist. It does not then concern either the living or the dead, since for the former it is not and the latter are no more.

Anyone who finds this passage compelling cannot but feel a sense of liberation: we should not fear living just because of an empty threat from death. Welcome as this liberation may seem, care must be taken of how we are to understand its proper implications. The Roman poet Lucretius (?94–55 BCE) wrote an epic work *De Rerum Natura* (On the Nature of Things) to expound the Epicurean philosophy; I shall use some passages from this work to give us something to get our teeth into, for only then can we uncover the rich assortment of philosophical issues raised by this position and see whether it is compelling.

Let us start with the following lines from Lucretius' poem:

> What has this bugbear Death to frighten Man,
> If Souls can die, as well as Bodies can?

We have, in these lines, assumption 1 of the Epicurean position: death means death. Some are quite easily seduced into a confused way of thinking about what it is like to be dead, which in turn leads to an understandable fear of being dead. This kind of confusion is illustrated by Rosencrantz in Tom Stoppard's play *Rosencrantz and Guildenstern Are Dead*:

> Do you ever think of yourself as actually dead, lying in a box with a lid on it? ... It's silly to be depressed by it. I mean one thinks of it like being alive in a box, one keeps forgetting to take into account the fact that one is dead.

The confusion comes from thinking of death as a state much like sleep or, at least, as a state of experiencing the tedium of eternally lying around doing nothing very interesting. But death is not like this. Death is not a kind of living. We can put it this way: we can quite rationally fear being in a state of having to experience the rest of time from a box in the ground. That would, indeed, be awful (and something it would be appropriate to get depressed about) but it is not our present concern. Our concern is not whether we should fear *life* after death (that is, life after the death of our biological body) but whether we can rationally fear *death* after death. Those who believe in the immortality of the soul may fear (or look forward to) life after biological death but those of us who do not believe that there is any way of sustaining life after the biological death of the body (given current technology) need to ask what it is about the state of death, the state of *non*-living, that can in any way be considered a harm, given that we cannot experience it.

Let us accept the assumption that death means death. This leads us to consider whether death in this sense can be considered a harm. Lucretius doesn't think so:

> And since the Man who *Is* not, feels not woe
> (For death exempts him and wards off the blow,
> Which we, the living, only feel and bear),
> What is there left for us in Death to fear?

The assumption underlying this passage is that we must *feel* something for it to be a harm. In other words, we have assumption 2: death is not something which can be experienced; so it cannot be either a harm or a benefit

It is one thing to say that being dead is not something that can be experienced and quite another to say that therefore it cannot be a harm. As Thomas Nagel argues, if we could only be harmed by things of which we were aware, then:

> [it] means that even if a man is betrayed by his friends, ridiculed behind his back and despised by people who treat him politely to his face, none of it can be counted as a misfortune for him so long as he does not suffer as a result. It means that a man is not injured if his wishes are ignored by the executor of his will or if, after his death, the belief becomes current that all the literary works on

which his fame rests were really written by his brother,
who died in Mexico at the age of twenty-eight.

(Nagel 1970: 4)

Robert Nozick (1997) also has a memorable example:

You have what you believe is a private relationship with
someone. However, unbeknownst to you, I am filming it
with my super-duper camera and sound equipment and
distributing the film to people whom you will never
encounter. Nothing in your life is changed by the fact
that people are packing the pornographic movie theaters
in Outer Mongolia to keep up with the latest serial instal-
ment in your life. So, should anyone care? And is the
only ground on which my action can be criticized, the
nature of all viewers' experience?

A natural response to such examples is to say that although
nobody *did* experience the harm, they *could* have done. This is
what makes them different from the case of death, which *could
never* be experienced as a harm. Some might argue that this does
not show that death is not a harm but that death is a *peculiar* kind
of harm; one that could never be experienced. This seems to me
to be the wrong response, for a number of reasons, the most
important of which is that it confuses the harm itself either with
the *effects* of the harm or with the *knowledge* of the harm. We can
make the point in this way: what *is* it to experience the harm of
someone talking about you behind your back? It seems to me
that if someone is talking about you behind your back, to you it
feels *no different* than if someone were not talking about you
behind your back. *This*, your current experience, is what it feels

like to be talked about behind your back. That's the nature of that particular harm – it is one that does not give rise to any change in the experience of the one harmed. If we found out about the harm, we would certainly feel different but this change in how we feel would be an *effect* of the harm (or rather, in this case, an effect of knowing about the harm); it isn't the harm itself.

When we fall off our bikes and break a rib, we feel excruciating pain: we can see this as an incontrovertible harm. But the harm done is the breaking of the rib, not the pain felt. The pain is an effect of breaking the rib. If we could somehow bypass the felt pain, we would still think harm had been done in breaking the rib (the painful effect of this harm *adds* to the unfortunate circumstances, rather than *exhausts* them). The correct response is to say that the issue over the actual or possible experience or knowledge of the harm is a red herring: there are clear cases of harms which need not be known about and need not (and sometimes cannot) be experienced; to think that experience or knowledge is important (or even possible) is to confuse the harm with its typical effects. Indeed, in some of these cases, that someone would feel harmed if they had found out about the harm rather *supports* the view that the person has been harmed when they were ignorant of it, since it *explains* the unpleasant feeling. As Nagel says: 'Loss, betrayal, deception and ridicule are [not] bad because people suffer when they learn of them ... The natural view is that the discovery of betrayal makes us unhappy because it is bad to be betrayed – not that betrayal is bad because its discovery makes us unhappy' (Nagel 1970: 5).

Far from having to be treated as an atypical harm, death can be treated on a par with these widely accepted harms – at least, there is no argument from considerations of the possible experience of harm which will stop it from being so treated. Nevertheless, it may be thought that death is different in that, unlike other harms, its *effects* do not give rise to an unpleasant experience (such as pain), since no experiences can be had when you're dead. In this sense, death is not like breaking a rib. But this hardly matters, because it *is* rather like harms where mere knowledge of the harm has such effects. I do not mean that we can know that we have died; certainly, we can't know that, but that doesn't stop us from knowing that we *will* die (and some can predict it with more accuracy than others). For some, knowledge that we will die has unpleasant effects, such as inducing feelings of melancholy or dread. That death cannot be experienced, then, is no bar to it being considered a harm just like many other harms.

This leaves us in a better position to tackle the next issue, which Lucretius expresses as:

For whosoe'er shall in misfortunes live,
Must *Be*, when those misfortunes shall arrive

There are a number of assumptions being made here, one being assumption 3: harms must be located near the one harmed.

It is useful to think of harm as a relation between the thing that does the harming and the thing which is harmed. If someone is run over by a bike, what does the harming is the running over by the bike and the thing harmed is the person in the road. In these cases, the running over is located at the same place and at the same time as the person who is run over (otherwise, the bike would have missed the person). Are all harms like this? Must the thing that does the harming always be near (in space and in time) the thing which is harmed?

Let's consider what I said about the relation between our death and our feeling of melancholy or dread. We should not think that it is the *later* death which *causes* the unpleasant feeling: to think this would be to hold that backwards causation was much more common than most people believe; that is, that an event that happens in 2010 can affect what happened in 1910. Rather, the more mundane but nevertheless correct way of thinking about it is that the *present* knowledge we have of our later death gives rise to the unpleasant feelings of dread and melancholy. The unpleasant feelings certainly occur at the same place and time as the harmed person's awareness of the harm but since it is not the melancholy that harms, but the death, this does not settle the issue of whether the thing which harms (the death) needs to occur at the same time and place as the harmed person. We need to ask, then, whether it is possible for the thing that harms to occur at a time where the harmed person is not, since if it can't, then nobody can be harmed by death; where death is, the living person isn't.

First, must the thing that harms occur at the same place as the thing harmed? Consider a person who paints a derogatory remark on the fuel tank of your beloved motorcycle. The damage is not just that done to the fuel tank but also to you, in potential damage to your reputation, humiliation, costing you money to respray, frustrating your desire to have an impeccable machine and violating your right to sole control of the things you own. The thing which does the harm, the painting on the motorcycle, harms you, the owner of the bike, whether or not you are located at the scene of the crime. You could be in Italy and the bike in England but you'd still be harmed by the event (whether or not you knew about it). Not being spatially located near the thing that harms does not stop you from being harmed.

Second, is time any different? Suppose that after our death, unflattering lies were circulated about us, our achievements were belittled and ridiculed and our final wishes never carried out. It seems to me that, just as in the case where we need not be located in the same place as the thing which harms, neither need we be located at the same time as the slanderous comments. The problem some have with this approach to events that happen after our death is that they think it involves some kind of backwards causation; that because the events which do the harming occur after the harmed person has died, the later events affect those which came earlier. However, we have seen that the relationship between the thing which harms, on the one hand, and the harmed person, on the other, need not be causal. It *might* be causal, in the sense that the obscene writing may cause you distress, which is a harm in itself, but the obscenity on the fuel tank does not *cause* the harm of having your rights and interests violated. Rather, there are certain conditions which must be upheld if our rights and interests are to remain intact; when those conditions do not hold, it *entails* that we have been harmed. So, we cannot rule out slander after our deaths being a harm on the grounds that it violates our idea of how causation works, since causation is neither here nor there. Rather, it is a good candidate for being a harm in so far as slander, whenever it occurs, is contrary to our interests.

This raises an interesting question: *which* person is harmed? As Lucretius says:

From sense of grief and pain we shall be free;
We shall not feel, because we shall not *Be*

This passage (as much as the passage from Lucretius before it) makes assumption 4: when we die, we no longer exist – there is no one to be harmed

Some think that the person ceases to exist after their death. But if the person no longer exists, then there *is* nobody who could be harmed after death. You can no more harm the non-existent dead than you can the tooth fairy. In so far as it is possible meaningfully to assess this, it seems to be the commonsense view that only the present exists, whereas the past, although it *did* exist, no longer does. According to this view, we are flesh and blood creatures in the way that Elizabeth I (1533–1603) is not. But if this view of the past is correct, it is not possible for Elizabeth I to be harmed by slurs on her reputation, for she doesn't exist!

Some do not subscribe to this view. According to them, Elizabeth I is as real, as much a flesh and blood creature, as we are; it is just that she is located at a time earlier than the one at which we are located. Given that we have already established that whether or not you can be harmed has nothing to do with when the thing which harms occurs, this view of the past quite clearly allows for Elizabeth I, in 1571, to be harmed, not just by a plot at that time to depose her but also by any unfair attempt made *now* inaccurately to change the history books to make her look rather unremarkable. The important issue is not the temporal relation between the harmful thing and the thing harmed but rather whether there *exists* someone to be harmed; in this view, there is.

Although this view about the past strikes many people as odd, there are good reasons, both from philosophy and from physics, for thinking that we should treat all times, past, present and future as equally real. These reasons can be complicated and cannot be discussed in any detail, since it would take us too far from our concerns in this book.[3] All that needs to be said is that, if we hold this view, there is nothing to stop us from thinking that dead people can be harmed after their death, since they remain in existence even though they are located in the past. The question to address is what must be said by those who reject this view of the past? Is it simply that the dead cannot be harmed?

Palle Yourgrau (1987) thinks that the dead can be harmed, even though they do not exist. He thinks that there are some things that do not exist; that is, things that, although they lack existence, are nevertheless not nothing. He states explicitly that we mustn't take him to mean that they exist in some special way; they are not like fictional characters or other abstract objects. A dead person, according to Yourgrau, is not a different kind of person from living, flesh and blood, people; they just differ in that they do not exist. I'm afraid that I find this position unintelligible, so let's not consider it further.

In saying that we should reject the idea of things that do not exist, should we also say that it is unintelligible to talk about things that *did* exist but no longer do? This is a difficult question in the philosophy of time; to say anything remotely satisfactory about it would take us too far away from our main concerns.[4] However, let us assume that we can make sense of it and consider the relatively unknown American, Sylvester Howard Roper (1823–1896). Is it at all possible to harm Roper now, in the way that the view that past people are just as real as we are allows? At first sight, it appears not – he doesn't exist – but let us consider

---

[3] Anyone who wishes to follow up this discussion of the nature of time should see my (2006a) book.

[4] See footnote 3.

a story from the history of the motorcycle. Although it is widely thought that the German automobile pioneer, Gottlieb Daimler (1834–1900), developed the first motorcycle in 1885, it is more accurate to say that Daimler developed the first gas-powered motorcycle to use the four-stroke internal combustion engine (the 'Otto Cycle Engine') invented by the engineer, Nicolaus August Otto, in 1876. However, Roper invented a two-cylinder coal-powered steam-engined motorcycle in 1867 which, if you allow your description of motorcycles to include steam engines, should be considered as the first motorcycle. Daimler's machine was much more important in the development of the motorcycle but Roper should have the credit for developing the first. He may even have been the first motorcycle fatality, since, in 1896, when he was seventy-three years old, he modified a motorcycle; travelling at 40mph (64km/h), he wobbled, fell off and was found dead at the scene. However, an autopsy revealed that he didn't die from the fall but from a heart attack.

Although this may go some way to putting the record straight, imagine that it's 1867 and you are Sylvester Howard Roper. You have just invented the motorcycle. You have an interest in being acknowledged as the inventor of this remarkable machine. Suppose that, a few hundred years in the future, it will be believed that you did not invent such a machine because someone in 2067 fabricated some evidence that seems to show conclusively that you couldn't have done. Whether or not you know, you, in 1867, have been harmed by what happens in 2067. If it is the case, in 1867, that you are harmed, it always will be the case that you are harmed in 1867. (If you were born in 1823, it always will be the case that you were born in 1823. To say anything else is contradictory.) In 2067 (and in subsequent years when schools teach that someone else, not Roper, developed the first motor-cycle), we can clearly say that Roper in 1867 was harmed by what happens in 2067, since we have already established that it is true that Roper in 1867 is harmed by what happens in 2067. None of this requires the existence of Roper in 2067.[5]

This story works if we assume certain things about the nature of time, such as that the future is 'fixed'. To say that the future is fixed is to say that there is already a fact about what will happen that makes all our statements about the future either true now or false now. If I now say 'I will go riding tomorrow', this is either true now or false now, depending on whether there is already a fact concerning tomorrow's riding. Those who believe that the future is as real as the present say that 'I will ride tomor-row' is either true now or false now, because facts already located in the future make it one or the other. Those who do not believe that the future already exists in this sense may, neverthe-less, say that 'I will ride tomorrow' is either true now or false now, because what will happen is fixed by the laws of nature that bring it about that I will ride tomorrow. Others might say that it is simply a brute fact now that something will happen.[6] These concepts of the future allow us to say that it is possible, in 1867, for 'Roper is harmed by what will happen' to be true.

However, if we think that the future does not exist and that no other facts could make statements about the future true, then what *will* happen in the future is not fixed. But if there is no fact, at that time, what will happen, then Roper could not possibly be harmed

---

[5] We may legitimately ask what, in 2067, makes it true that *in 1867 Roper was harmed by what happened in 2067* but this has a complicated answer. Nevertheless, one can be given. See my (2006a) book.

[6] I criticise these views in my (2006a) book.

by it. Similarly, we might think, not that there is *no* future but that there is no *particular* future; in other words, that the future 'branches'. If there is no particular future, just many ways in which the future could develop, then what will happen is not fixed at that time. At that time, Roper could not possibly be harmed by it. It looks like Roper cannot be harmed by things that happen after he has ceased to be, since at any time at which he exists, there is never any fact concerning what in the future he is harmed by.

There is, then, a complex relationship between whether you can be harmed after your death and the nature of time. Whether Roper's dramatic death was a harm for Roper depends on whether the sentence 'Roper is harmed by what will happen' can ever be true and that depends on whether facts about the future exist. This is a rather surprising conclusion. Given that it is not logically impossible to be immortal, it cannot be ruled out that we could live forever. So, it is not fixed now whether we will die or not and thus it is never true, so long as Roper exists, that there will be something in his future, such as his death, which can be said to harm him. It can never be true to say 'Roper is harmed by his death in 1896', since his death will always be in his future and when it arrives – that is, when it becomes a fact that he dies – he will no longer exist.[7]

Perhaps there is a different way of treating the situation. We might say that when the death, the fabrication of the evidence, or

[7] Those tempted to say that it can be true in 1895 that Roper will die because we are evaluating this relative to all of his *physically possible* futures (where it is not possible that he is immortal) and not the wider set of his logically possible futures (where it is possible that he is immortal), will have trouble explaining what 'physically possible' means. If it means something like it conforms to the laws of nature, as I show in my (2006a) book, what the laws of nature are is indeterminate, according to this view, and so cannot help here.

whatever it is that is taken to be the harm occurs, conditions then exist that are incompatible with the interests that Roper *had*. So, although it is never strictly true to say that *Roper* is harmed by these conditions, their existence is, in some sense, incompatible with his interests: that is, with the interests he had at a given time. This may well be good enough to say that we should avoid violating these interests, even though nobody is, strictly speaking, harmed by such a violation. We do, after all, think it legitimate to carry on some-one's good work or refrain from doing something out of respect for what they believed in. But this is quite different from saying that such a person is harmed by not respecting their interests.

So whether or not someone can be harmed after they have died depends on the nature of the future, since if there is now no fact concerning what will happen, nobody now can be harmed by it. And if you think, as I do, that we cannot tell whether the future is like this or not, because it could be either way (see Bourne 2006a), there is no way of telling whether people can be harmed after they have died. I find this very surprising but, since I cannot see a flaw in my argument, I find it entirely compelling. (However, time plays a part in the next assumption; for that purpose I shall assume that the future is 'fixed' and so people can be harmed by what happens in their future.)

The last issue to tackle concerning whether death can be seen as a harm can be captured by the following lines from Lucretius:

For, as before our Birth we felt no Pain
…
When once that pause of life has come between,
'Tis just the same as we had never been.

Underlying these thoughts is assumption 5: just as we do not fear the time before our birth, we should not fear the time after our death.

It may well be true that none of us fear the time before our birth, but this does not show that we should not fear the time after our death and still less does it show that the time of our non-existence before our birth cannot be considered a harm.[8] Suppose, for instance, that you fear your beloved motorcycle will be stolen while you are on holiday. And suppose that while on holiday, the bike is indeed stolen. How should you feel when you discover the news on your return? You might feel angry, depressed or many other emotions, but it would be inappropriate to *fear* the past event of someone stealing your motorcycle. Nevertheless, it would not follow that you should not have feared the stealing of the bike before you went on holiday. Further, the fact that you do not fear the stealing after it has been carried out does not show that it is, therefore, not a harm. Similarly, just because we do not fear the time before we were born, it doesn't follow that it wasn't a harm.

This is not quite the conclusion we want. Presumably we want an account that will explain why we think that the stealing was a harm but that the time before our conception was not, yet also explains our intuition that non-existence after life deserves a different emotional response to non-existence before life. Once we have an account to explain this intuition, we will be in

---

[8] Those who, because of their view of the nature of time, do not think we come into existence at the beginning of our lives and go out of existence at the end, can reformulate 'past non-existence of a person P' as 'earlier times not located by person P' and 'future non-existence of a person P' as 'later times not located by person P'.

a better position to see whether it has been vindicated or shown to be irrational.

Some might say that the reason it is legitimate to fear the motorcycle being stolen before it happens, but not afterwards, is because you do not *know* beforehand that it will be stolen. Fear, they might claim, is appropriate when we lack knowledge. Indeed, this is the only way plausibly to claim that we can legitimately fear past events. Think, for instance, of those times when you don't hear from somebody you are expecting and you fear that they have had a crash. It doesn't sound quite right to claim that what we fear is not a past event – the crash – but rather the future *knowledge* that they have had a crash. But whether or not we think we can fear past events, if fear is only appropriate when we lack knowledge, then since we do know that we will die, it is unlike the case of the stolen motorcycle. We need to find an example that works. Take the case of a trip to the dentist: if we do not fear a dentist appointment that we know occurred in the past, it doesn't follow that we should not fear a dentist appointment in the future – plenty of people fear such a thing, in the full knowledge of what will happen. Thus, although fear often goes with a lack of knowledge, we can fear things that we know of and about. The same goes for fearing our non-existence.

So, assumption 5 is invalid: it might be inappropriate to fear a past event or state of affairs of a certain kind (especially if you know about it) but that does not show that it is inappropriate to fear a future event or state of affairs of that kind (even if you know about it). Assumption 5 may, however, be nothing more than helpful advice, urging people not to think of death as an experience of disembodied existence (that is, to fear what it will be like to be dead): nobody experiences being dead, any more than anyone experiences life before conception, so if you fear non-existence after life *solely because* you think it is different from non-existence before life, this is the assumption you need to set you straight. But I, for one, am well aware that a state of non-existence is a state of non-existence, whether before or after life, yet it seems to me that it is legitimate to have different attitudes towards each. However, it needs to be shown why.

First, we need to refocus our discussion. Rather than phrase matters in terms of what is bad about non-existence, we should concentrate on what is good about being alive. For a normal human, most people agree that, in general, it is better to have had a longer rather than a shorter life (so long as it was worthwhile). This in itself does not distinguish the harm of death from the time before we were alive, since if more life is better than less life, the time of non-existence before being alive is as much a harm as being dead, since neither allows for more living. One influential response to this is to say that, although we could die at any time, we could not have been born at any other time, for anybody born at a different time from the time at which we were born could not have been us but a different person. The contemporary American philosopher, Saul Kripke, argues that a person's origins are an essential feature of that person. He writes: 'How could a person originating from different parents, from a totally different sperm and egg, be *this very woman*? ... could *this table* have been made from a completely *different* block of wood or even of water cleverly hardened into ice ...?' (Kripke 1980: 113). Along similar lines, Nagel argues:

> ... we cannot say that the time prior to a man's birth is time in which he would have lived had he been born not

then but earlier. For aside from the brief margin permit-
ted by premature labour, he could not have been born
earlier: anyone born substantially earlier than he was
would have been someone else. Therefore, the time prior
to his birth is not time in which his subsequent birth
prevents him from living. His birth, when it occurs, does
not entail the loss to him of any life whatever.

(Nagel 1970: 8)

This is not quite right. Nagel runs together the *time* at which
someone came into existence and their *origin*. Suppose we
think that Kripke is right to think that the origin (that is, the
particular sperm and egg coupling) is essential to the identity of
a person, there is no reason to think, as Nagel does, that the *time*
is essential. First, if all that matters is that the person originated
from that sperm and that egg, what is the argument for thinking
that the sperm and egg could not have existed earlier? Second, if
the sperm and egg were frozen, then so long as the person originated from them, the person could have been brought into
existence much later. Suppose that in the future (when the technology is reliable enough) a couple who froze their sperm and
egg thirty years before decide to bring a child into existence
from them. Fifteen years later, when that child is formulating
plans for their future, it becomes apparent that the world will
soon be coming to an end, due to a nuclear war. Supposing it
was a more-or-less arbitrary decision of the parents to bring the
child into existence at that time – that in fact they had had
enough money, job security and what-not to have the child at
any time during the period the egg and sperm were frozen – is it
not right to say that the child has been harmed by this period of

non-existence? Had they been brought into existence earlier, they would have had the chance to do what the adult it could have been could have done. There are conceivable situations, then, where the time before our existence could be considered a harm. The actual time at which we are born is neither here nor there, unless it is the only time at which our origins, such as the particular sperm and egg, can exist.

If it isn't Nagel's considerations about time that explain the harm of death, what does? Given that we *are* alive, the good feature of having more life is that it facilitates our doing those things we value; so death is a harm, in putting an end to all that. There is nothing intrinsically bad about not being alive, any more than there is anything intrinsically good about being alive: life is valuable only in so far as it is instrumental in achieving those ends which *are* of instrinsic value, such as being creative, learning new things, forming relationships with people and so on, whereas death is only bad in so far as it thwarts these plans.[9] This is why we view the death of someone in the prime of life as more of a tragedy than when it happens to an elderly person who has had the opportunity to do all these things. Of course, this is all relative to what is normal for a human being. A race of people who normally lived as long as the biblical Methuselah (reported to have lived 969 years), would probably deem tragic even the long and productive life of the English philosopher Bertrand Russell (1872–1970).

---

[9] Everything I have said is compatible with life itself having intrinsic as well as instrumental value. In this view, having more of life, however it treats you, is better than less. I have not shown that this is wrong, I just find it incredible that anyone could believe that life could be good independent of how it is lived. What would be valuable in a life where you have no friends, have severely debilitating migraine pain all day long and regularly vomit faeces?

The time before our existence, in the normal case, does not thwart our projects and so cannot be seen to be a harm in the same way; but there is nothing, in principle, against considering the time of non-existence before our lives to be harmful if it really did stop us from carrying out our projects. It is just that, in the normal case, it doesn't; we are perfectly right not to take such a period of non-existence to be a harm. Viewing life in this way is a nice explanation both of the harm of death and the (factual although not in principle) asymmetry between the non-existence after life and non-existence before life.

Death (along with other things that occur after life) is something which can be said to be a harm for the one who dies. I want to continue living because I have certain things I want to do. If I don't get to do them because I die, then death harms *me*, the *living* person who has those plans. We shouldn't think of death (or things that happen after death) as harming a dead person. That seems to me to be incoherent. But I suspect that this concept of death is what troubles those who have reservations about donating their organs after they die. I hope that people will see, if they didn't before, that being dead is not a kind of living; that you do not need your organs after you have died and so it can hardly harm your interests for someone to take them to save someone who does need them. Until the time comes when more people see that we should adopt a default policy of just taking bodily organs from those who have died, we should all be prepared voluntarily to donate them – especially since motorcycle accidents are an obvious source of organs for transplant.

This chapter has concentrated on the nature of our *non-existence*. The next obvious question is: what is the nature of *existence*?

Image 2. Trinity virtually (?) riding a genuine (?) Ducati 998 in *Matrix Reloaded* (2003)

Second Gear

The nuts and bolts of existence

> What we first hear is never noises or complexes of sounds
> but the creaking wagon, the motorcycle.
>
> Martin Heidegger, *Being and Time*

We have, in this statement, a key ingredient of a solution to a deep philosophical problem: what is the nature of existence? Although many philosophers have concerned themselves with questions that are very general in scope and in some way ultimate, the nature of existence will strike many readers as a strange and difficult issue. We can ask straightforward questions about the nature of humans, or money, or jelly and get relatively straightforward answers, but where do we begin to give an answer to the question of the nature of existence? Luckily for us, one proposed answer – again, by the existentialists – is right under our noses and can be grasped by reflecting on the experience of motorcycling. If we were of the melodramatic existentialist persuasion, we might even formulate a battle-cry of our own: *the biker holds the key to understanding our existence; the biker is the ultimate existential hero.* What exactly would lead us to say this?

THE *METHOD*, THE *MEDITATIONS* AND THE *MATRIX*

Can you be sure that you are not a brain floating in a vat of liquid, attached to a computer operated by a scientist, which feeds you all your thoughts and experiences, such as the experience that you are reading a book? Or, as the brilliant comedian Armando Iannucci once put it, how do we know that we're not part of a big World Wide Web, created by God, in danger of being turned off at any minute when he decides to go back to doing some work? If you cannot be certain that you are not a brain in a vat (or lost in God's internet), how can you be certain of anything? How do we know that the world as we take it to be is not entirely different from how it really is? This is the situation in which those in *Matrix Reloaded* (2003), for instance, find themselves.

This idea is far from new and was first posed in this form by the French philosopher-mathematician-scientist, René Descartes (1596–1650). In his book *Meditations* (1641), Descartes argues that we cannot simply appeal to our senses to guarantee us knowledge of the world, since, 'from time to time I have found that the senses deceive and it is prudent never to trust completely those who have deceived us even once'. Even when we seem to be in a situation where mistakes are unlikely (such as in good lighting or where the objects in which we are interested are reasonably close), Descartes does not think we can simply appeal to our senses, since we could be dreaming: 'I plainly see that there are never any sure signs by means of which being awake can be distinguished from being asleep.' In any case, even if my present experiences can be taken to be reliable, there are certain things I think I know that don't depend on present experiences, such as the general truth that all triangles have three sides and three interior angles that add up to 180°.[1] After a few more musings, Descartes concludes: 'I am finally compelled to admit that there is not one of my former beliefs about which a doubt may not properly be raised.' Because it is very difficult honestly to stop believing these things, he introduces the device of the evil demon: 'I will suppose ... some evil demon of the utmost power and cunning has employed all his energies in order to deceive me.' To a considerable extent, having the evil demon on the scene eases the pressure placed on us by having to follow through Descartes' method of systematically doubting everything of which we cannot be certain, since it is *very* difficult to doubt how things seem to you; very difficult, that is, to doubt that there is a book in front of you when you can see it and feel it and so on. But it is much easier to doubt that what *seems* to you to be the way things are *is* the way that things are, beyond how it seems. This is what the evil demon allows you to do, which makes it a very powerful tool.

However, Descartes did not want to show that we could not be sure of anything; quite the opposite. He tried to show how our knowledge could be based on firm foundations that could

---

[1] However, this is only true of triangles in 'flat', Euclidean space. Triangles in a positively curved space, such as on the surface of a sphere, have interior angles which sum to more than 180° and triangles in a negatively curved space, such as on the surface of a saddle, sum to less than 180°.

not be doubted. The first step in his project is one of the most well-known philosophical arguments ever put forward:

> Let [the evil demon] deceive me as much as he can, he will never bring it about that I am nothing so long as I think that I am something ... I must finally conclude that this proposition, *I am, I exist*, is necessarily true whenever it is put forward by me or conceived in my mind.

Or, as he more famously put it in his earlier book, *Discourse on Method* (1637), 'I think, therefore I am.'

Although this looks like a compelling argument to prove that at least one thing exists when it thinks that it does, namely the thinking thing itself, it is not clear that this is enough to serve as a foundation for the rest of our knowledge. Unfortunately, we cannot discuss the problems here, since the possible routes we could take, either by patching up Descartes' attempt or by starting from an entirely different place, are many and varied. It would take a whole book to discuss properly just this one issue. Nevertheless, there is one route – the 'existentialist' route – which stands out as being particularly relevant to motorcyclists; so this is the one we shall travel.

HOW TO USE TOOLS

The impression we are left with when we follow Descartes' method is that how things seem in our experience does not give us *direct* access to the world beyond but is rather more like a veil, which allows us, at best, only to make *inferences* about what is on the other side. Nevertheless, we do have direct access to our conscious experiences; and it is this fact that the German philosopher, Edmund Husserl (1859–1938), thought was the key to grounding our knowledge of the nature of things.[2] Whether or not the objects actually exist, we certainly take our experiences to be *about* those things; by reflecting on our conscious experience and trying to describe it, we uncover the structure of taking our experiences to be about those things.

There are numerous conflicting interpretations of the significance of this project that we need not mention. What is worth pointing out is that we can see this as part of the tradition that starts with reflecting on our conscious experience and seeing where it gets us. This tradition assumes a particular view of our relationship with the world, where we, the subjects, are set apart from objects. We look around us and see chairs and tables as distinctly separate from us; there is, so to speak, a 'gap' between us and the table. It is this gap that feeds our concern over whether and how we can bridge it. We wonder whether what we, as subjects, experience in any way resembles what is on the other side of the gap, if indeed there *is* anything. For instance, it seems to me that I am looking through a window onto a car park in which there is a Ducati motorcycle. But the Ducati is 'other' than I. So how can I be sure that the thing 'out there' exists?

Despite this being a rather intuitive way of understanding our relationship with the world, the existentialist approach questions whether it captures the most fundamental way in which we are related. Existentialists deny that our primary relationship is as a subject related to a world of objects. The German philosopher, Martin Heidegger (1889–1976), in his

[2] See Husserl (1900–1).

book *Being and Time* (1927) claims that our relationship is more like the following: consider the motorcycle. When we are riding it, we don't think about it as an object; we just ride it. We change gear (often not only without realising which gear we are in but also without being aware that we are changing gear at all). We brake, accelerate, pull in the clutch, lean the bike when cornering and perform a host of actions of which we have no conscious awareness. Essentially, our motorcycle is a *tool*. And like any tool, we engage with it primarily as being useful for a purpose; we might, for instance, take it to have an impressive capacity for acceleration or to be good at cornering but uncomfortable for passengers. When we *use* it for this purpose, we do not consider it consciously as an object; what we do is *cope* with the motorcycle and our coping need not involve any conscious awareness. The motorcycle, in Heidegger's terminology, is 'ready-to-hand'.

The point of emphasising this kind of interaction with the world, according to existentialists, is that for such an interaction to be possible, we must get our hands dirty; we must *already* be involved in the workings of the world. Scepticism about the external world is thus avoided, since the sceptical questions don't get a look in, for they arise as a result of taking the motorcycle as being an object with certain properties, such as its shape and its colour, from which we *infer* its existence. As soon as we have to infer the existence of such an object from the experiences that we have, a gap opens up between us and the object, into which doubt can creep. In the existentialist view of our relationship with the world, there is no such *inference* from the properties we experience the motorcycle as having to the motorcycle's existence, for, as Heidegger's quote at the beginning of the chapter asserts: 'What we first hear is never noises or complexes of sounds but ... the motorcycle.'

We do not *infer* the existence of objects but rather *use* them directly and this in turn implies other things; for motorcycles have significance for us only against a background of other things, such as that most motorcycles require roads. The existence of roads implies those who built them and the places joined by them, which in turn imply other things. Motorcycles also have to be set against a background of skills, such as slipping the clutch, a skill that was taught and thus a skill which implies those who taught it. A web of practices, such as safety and traffic regulations, is invoked when we consider the motorcycle as 'ready-to-hand'; these in turn presuppose a host of factors necessary for their existence. We participate in a shared and social way of living. Being a coping being presupposes other beings with whom to exercise such skills and engage in such activities.

So, although we can and do ask questions about the external world and the objects in it (including questions about minds other than our own), this stance is only possible against the background of our practical involvement in the world and everything that brings with it. From characterising our relationship to the motorcycle in terms of using a tool, we can, so to speak, bring much more of the world back into existence than if we start from Descartes' position.

But from where do we get the idea that the motorcycle is 'other' than us, which leads us to the view of ourselves as subjects in a world of objects, which in turn invites the sceptical questions? According to existentialists, it happens like this: suppose we are riding the motorcycle. We use it as a tool, with no conscious awareness of the various things we are doing. As we approach a corner, we drop down a couple of gears and start to turn. We notice that it doesn't feel quite right as we lean. We are no longer coping with the motorcycle. We realise that we have knocked the gear into neutral, that we've effectively lost power and that we'll be on the floor if we don't do something. At this point, we consciously direct our attention to the problem and the motorcycle becomes an object of our consciousness. In Heidegger's terminology, the motorcycle changes from being 'ready-to-hand' to 'unready-to-hand'. Thus, this kind of awareness of the object is one stage removed from our primary interaction with it. Heidegger's point is that accounting for our knowledge of the world by focusing on this kind of conscious awareness of objects (as Husserl does) does not get to the heart of the matter; it doesn't capture the most basic way in which we encounter the world.

If the 'unready-to-hand' is one stage removed from our primary way of interacting with the world, the traditional philosophical and scientific concept of our relationship is one stage even further removed. The 'unready-to-hand' arises from a conscious awareness of a problem with the 'ready-to-hand' but has rather a practical flavour – we have to *do* something about getting this motorcycle round the corner instead of dropping it and ourselves in the road. Traditionally, what philosophers and scientists do is *contemplate* these objects, independent of our concern with them as tools. The objects are seen as things with properties about which we can reason, and on which we can conduct experiments. In Heidegger's terminology, when we take this contemplative stance towards the world, the motorcycle becomes 'present-at-hand'. It is at this level that sceptical worries arise; although, according to Heidegger, it is still important to investigate objects at this level, it is nevertheless two stages removed from our primary interaction with objects, so it's the wrong place to start if we are to investigate the nature of the most fundamental level of existence. If, however, we start from the level of the 'ready-to-hand' – from a position of already being in the world – scepticism, so the argument goes, vanishes. This looks like a rather attractive solution to countering scepticism about the external world.

A SPANNER IN THE WORKS

Heidegger's work is notoriously vague and suspiciously cryptic, as are many existentialist writings. Nevertheless, I have presented what I take to be an interesting position in its own right and in the spirit of existentialism, whether or not it is an entirely accurate reflection of any one existentialist writer. Now that we have a clear position to work with, we need to consider it critically. Does it show that scepticism has been refuted? And if not, is there anything important it does show?

First, we should note that, despite the claim that our primary relationship with the world is at the level of the 'ready-to-hand', this doesn't accord with much of our experience. We often encounter objects without knowing how to use them or even what they are used for; indeed, many aren't used for anything. We have to learn how to use them and, more often than not, the objects will begin as 'unready-to-hand'. This more or less describes my first (practical) encounters with the motorcycle.[3] Not being a driver, it took me a while to grasp what the clutch

---

[3] However, my first encounter really seems to fit more within the contemplative 'present-at-hand' stage, as I note in the final chapter. Either way, my first encounter doesn't fit the 'ready-to-hand' stage.

was meant to do. Indeed, at this stage, it would be an understatement to call the motorcycle 'unready-to-hand' – it was *completely alien*! It is only after quite a few rides that the motorcycle even remotely approaches the 'ready-to-hand', where we can cope without any awareness of it. Calling the 'ready-to-hand' stage our primary way of interacting with things in the world is misleading – it neglects just how much of an achievement it is to get there; to get over the 'unready-to-hand' stage.[4] So, although this doesn't necessarily show that our primary interaction with objects is the reverse of the existentialist's, with the 'ready-to-hand' being two stages removed from the more fundamental 'present-to-hand', it does cast doubt on the idea that any stage can be taken to be more fundamental than another.

Second, and more important, it isn't clear that acknowledging the 'ready-to-hand' stage is enough to avoid scepticism anyway. Scepticism usually arises from questioning how or whether you know *that* something is the case: how do we know *that* there is a motorcycle in front of us; how do we know *that* the properties we take a thing to have are a true representation of how the thing really is and so on. Resting our case on the sole basis that things seem to be that way is not a sufficient justification for inferring that things are that way. We could, for instance, be in a computer simulation.

There are many accounts of this kind of knowledge and how they respond to the sceptical challenge, far too many to be able to discuss in detail. But we can roughly characterise most

---

[4] The word 'primary' is ambiguous in meaning between *first* encounter and *fundamental* encounter. Nevertheless, it is not clear that the 'ready-to-hand' is primary in either case.

accounts by saying that we know, for instance, that my motor-cycle is yellow if and only if it is *true* that it is yellow (we can't know things which are false), we *believe* that it is yellow and we have some *justification* for believing that it is yellow (it can't just be a fluke that we believe something to be true).[5] Such a jus-tification might be that we can cite reasons for believing it; or we might think that so long as the methods we are using to gen-erate our beliefs are reliable (for instance, that visual perception is a way of gaining true beliefs), then this is sufficient justifica-tion to render our true beliefs knowledge.

Giving an account of this kind of knowledge has been one of the major projects of philosophy since the Ancient Greeks. What the existentialist solution to scepticism attempts to do is to bypass the worry about this kind of knowledge of the world by saying that there is a more fundamental knowledge that we have where the sceptical problems do not arise. The difference between these two different kinds of knowledge can be brought out explicitly, again by considering the motorcycle. You may know everything that there is to know *about* riding a motor-cycle, such as to know *that* you have to balance, to know *that* you have to use the clutch to change gear, to know *that* you lean with the motorcycle into corners. But all this kind of knowledge could be learned from a book; it could be known without even

---

[5] Although this has been disputed. For instance, we might say that a school-child who is reluctant to answer a particular question, but who gives the correct answer when prodded by a teacher, knows the answer but does not believe it. However, these cases are perhaps best described by saying that they do believe it – since they do give that answer – it's just that they may not believe that they believe it or, even better, that they don't fully believe it and the costs of getting the wrong answer (embarrassment in front of classmates or some such) are so great as to affect what would otherwise be a fairly confident response.

getting onto a motorcycle. Yet, as we all know, it is one thing knowing the facts and quite another getting on the motorcycle and *doing* it. In other words, we may know everything there is to know *about* riding a motorcycle, without knowing *how* to ride one. In emphasising our primary relationship to things in the world as being of *using* them as *tools* rather than of contemplating *that* they are a certain way, existentialists in effect assert that know-how is a more fundamental kind of knowledge than know-that and since know-how presupposes our being in the world, scepticism is bypassed.

Neat as this manoeuvre is, it cannot be the end of the story. Consider *Matrix Reloaded*: as Trinity rides a Ducati 998 against the flow of traffic (see Image 2), from her perspective the motorcycle will be 'ready-to-hand'. She certainly uses the motorcycle as a tool and she certainly knows how to ride it but she's effectively in a computer simulation. How, then, does the fact that objects are 'ready-to-hand' bypass scepticism? If we are in a simulation, what we know is how to ride a *virtual motorcycle*; this object's being 'ready-to-hand' for us, with everything that implies (virtual roads, virtual people and so on) obviously does not avoid scepticism or show us anything about how things really are with genuine motorcycles, genuine people and genuine roads, if such there be.

The obvious response is to say that the very possibility of our being able to conceptualise the idea of being in a computer simulation relies on our having know-how of things in this world. But it is hard to see why it must. Trinity will say, of herself, that she can ride a Ducati 998. We know that Trinity has, so far, only displayed knowledge of how to virtually ride a virtual Ducati 998. *We* can distinguish the virtual Ducati 998 from what we can call the 'genuine Ducati 998' because we know Trinity is in a computer simulation. But why should the fact that what we call the 'genuine Ducati 998' is 'ready-to-hand' for us show that we are not in a computer simulation for someone who knows how to *genuinely* genuinely ride a *genuine* genuine Ducati 998?

Knowing how to virtually ride a virtual Ducati 998 does not show that we know how to genuinely ride a genuine Ducati 998, any more than knowing how to fly in a dream means that we know how to fly when we wake up. But knowing how to virtually ride and knowing how to genuinely ride may well employ the same skills. That is why people use flight simulators to learn how to pilot aeroplanes, since if the skills learned when virtually flying were not the same as when genuinely flying, virtual flying would be no more than a way to pass the time. (This is unlike knowing how to fly in a dream, because no matter how hard I will myself to do it – which is the only flying skill I've found you need in dreams – I never seem to get anywhere near as far off the ground in real life as I'd like.) So, even if we concede, for the sake of argument, that our primary knowledge is know-how, this still cannot, in itself, establish that the tools we are using are genuine tools rather than virtual tools.

We cannot undermine these thought experiments, then, by saying that the notion of a simulation only works against the background of having the real thing. This may well be true at some level but it does not show that *we* are the ones who are not deceived. Scepticism only requires a *contrast*. We know the computer simulation people are deluded with the same qualitative experience as we have; so how do we know that we are not in a similar position with respect to someone who is controlling our environment? My point is not that we should be worried that we are in a computer simulation. The point is that just from invoking the idea of the 'ready-to-hand', scepticism has not been shown to have been undermined. If we want to avoid scepticism, we'll have to take a different route.

Perhaps the solution *does* lie in Heidegger: 'What we first hear is never noises or complexes of sounds but the creaking wagon, the motorcycle', but lies in a different direction to that in which he took it. What he is really getting at is that when we perceive objects, we perceive the objects *directly*; we don't make an *inference* from particular colours and shapes to the existence of chairs and tables; we just see the chairs and tables. If that is what we need, then it is not necessary also to argue that our primary way of knowing about the world is through know-how; we might just conclude that we know *that* something is the case through direct perception. I won't, however, expand on this thought here since, unlike the existential solution, it is catered for elsewhere in introductory text books (see, for example, Dancy 1985) and also unlike the existential solution to scepticism, it doesn't have much of a link to motorcycle riding.

Does this mean we have wasted our time in considering the existential approach? No, for although we need not go along with the existentialists in thinking that know-how is a more fundamental knowledge than know-that – that practical knowledge is more fundamental than knowledge of facts – we may still think, as I do, that both kinds of knowledge are equally important in giving a proper account of our understanding of the world. That was worth pointing out. It is not possible fully to understand the world without engaging with it in a practical way: we can't learn everything from books. In this respect, the existentialists are perfectly correct in thinking that the kind of knowledge with which science deals does not exhaust all kinds of knowledge, but they have not yet made the case for thinking that all knowledge rests on know-how. Rather, it is much more plausible to think that the different kinds of knowledge complement each other in our understanding of the world.

ZEN AND THE ART OF MOTORCYCLE MAINTENANCE

We have seen that the existentialist claims that our fundamental relationship with the world is of practical engagement with it. Some will be struck by just how similar this emphasis is to the attitude adopted in Robert Pirsig's *Zen and the Art of Motorcycle Maintenance*. Zen Buddhism and existentialism are in many ways worlds apart but there is a theme which they share: the attempt to overcome and dissolve various 'dualisms'.

In Zen Buddhism, the world as it really is is not how we take it to be. Distinctions between various things only exist because humans impose their classifications on things; the world is not 'ready-carved'.[6] *We* divide our motorcycle into its various parts; there is no real distinction between them. There is no real distinction between the motorcycle and the road, nor between the motorcycle and ourselves. In reality, there is no distinction between one human and another – even that distinction is imposed on the world. The subject-object dualism that we saw the existentialist trying to overcome and dissolve by bridging the gap between us and the world is something that Zen Buddhism also tries to overcome and dissolve, for it is an

---

[6] For an interesting defence of this concept of the world (as well as more on the brain in a vat hypothesis) see Putnam (1981).

illusion: there is no difference between the subject and the object in the world as it really is.

There are, however, differences in the two positions. First, their methodologies are different: existentialists achieve their conclusion through philosophical reflection; Zen Buddhists achieve it through meditation. Second, and more importantly, the kind of dissolution of the subject-object dualism that existentialism arrives at does not result in a world that is an undifferentiated 'blob' in the way that Zen Buddhism does but rather overcomes our separation from the world by putting us back *in* it, by emphasising the tool-like nature of being rather than the thing-like nature.

Nevertheless, the parallels remain. 'Don't think, just ride. Lean with the bike; be one with the bike.' Is this an expression of the existentialist's view of our fundamental relationship with the world or is it the Zen Buddhist's advice? I'll leave that as a rhetorical question, because I want to take this discussion in a more interesting direction.[7] The concept of the world that is opened up by the dissolution of various dualisms (between our selves and the world, between our minds and our bodies, between our selves and others) requires a radical rethinking of the nature of things. Let us consider the nature of the self.

PEEPING TOM AND THE SHED AT THE BOTTOM OF THE GARDEN

Existentialists do not deny that there are such things as motorcycles; it is just that they claim that they are not primarily to be

[7] Those interested in following up the Zen side of things should see Priest (2006).

thought of as inert, *thing-like*, entities but rather, a means of allowing you to *do* something. Yet they do try to give an account of where the concept of the thing-like nature of objects comes from and the same kind of strategy carries over to the case of our selves. This is best approached by using one of Sartre's examples. Consider a man – let's call him Tom – who, out of curiosity, peeps through a keyhole and listens at a door. He is totally absorbed in what he is doing, is not reflecting on his situation and so is not conscious of his self. He hears the stairs creak behind him. He realises that someone is there watching him. He suddenly becomes aware of himself. He suddenly becomes an object for the gaze of another.

The experience that we first consider in this example is entirely directed towards whatever it was that was carrying on on the other side of the door. Tom only became aware of himself as a subject, as the thing having the thoughts, when there was an awareness of the awareness of another. Under the gaze of another, the *activity* at the keyhole that was directed towards the events on the other side of the door is forced to become determinately *thing-like*. So even though, according to Sartre, our real selves are primarily more like an *activity* than a *thing*, we have here an account of where the traditional idea of our thing-like selves comes from. The nice feature of this account, according to Sartre, is that it is a proof that other minds exist, for given that we do think of ourselves as thing-like, then it must be because we are subject to the gaze of another. Another sceptical gap – between our selves and other selves – has been bridged.

We cannot get into a critical assessment of this argument but there is a striking feature of this position that is worth commenting on: that how we think of ourselves depends on matters that are *external* to us. We ordinarily think of ourselves as free-standing, isolated units but, according to this view, we would not think like this were it not for the existence of other things.

To some, this may sound strange but it can be seen to figure in an account of a slightly different aspect of the nature of a thing than the one we have just discussed; that is, in accounting for how something can remain the same thing from day to day. We touched on the case of the identity of a person at the end of the first chapter but let us consider the identity of things in general. The motorcycle serves as a good example. You notice one day that your bike – let's call it Horace – is having trouble starting. You change the spark plugs but still have no luck getting the bike started. Then you spot some fouling on the spark plug, realise that the fuel mix is too rich and so you probably need to change the air filter. The bike starts but you notice that the brakes aren't as responsive as they were and the back tyre loses traction when cornering. They too need changing, as do the sprockets and chain, the broken clutch lever, the misted-up head light and the rest. You change these and would say that Horace was the better for it. Nevertheless, you've had the bike a few years and so want to replace much of the bodywork with some carbon fibre upgrades. You spend every spare weekend for a year devoted to the project. Each weekend, Horace looks better and better. You replace the mirrors with some stylish ones that fit on the ends of the handlebars. You replace the wheels, install some high-tech suspension and fit new exhaust pipes. I think it is intuitive to say that, after all of these changes, Horace would be in particularly good shape and looking better than ever.

But what makes Horace the same bike today as it was a few years ago? Most of its original parts have been upgraded and it looks nothing like the bike that came from the factory, yet we still seem to have a firm grip on the idea of what it is to remain the same thing over time. There is some kind of connection between each stage of the bike's upgrade, such that we say that it is the same bike throughout the process. However, suppose that, in the shed at the bottom of the garden, you kept all of the parts that you replaced. And suppose that your friend put them all together and added a new engine. What would you say then, if your friend were to claim that, using the parts kept in the shed, he'd rebuilt Horace from scratch? Would you say that he can't have rebuilt Horace because *this* is Horace (pointing to your beloved upgrade)? Suppose another friend were to come along who hadn't seen Horace since before any of its parts had been replaced. Is there anything that can be said to convince her that one of these bikes is Horace and the other isn't? Should she say that Horace has new bodywork and so on, and so side with you or should she say that Horace has a new engine, and so side with your friend? Perhaps she should say that *part* of Horace is located in one bike and the other part located in the other bike (because she equates Horace with the original parts). But suppose that all the parts of Horace had, one by one, been discarded after being replaced. My intuition in this case is to say that Horace has had a complete make-over, rather than that Horace no longer exists, even though there are no parts left from the original bike.

In the case of the one bike, even when there is a change of all the parts (so long as it wasn't an instantaneous change of all its parts), it seems clear that it is still Horace. In the case of the two bikes, I intuitively feel pulled in all the proposed directions; it is not clear that there is a fact concerning which one is

Horace. This seems to show that whether we count something at one time as the same thing at a different time will, in part, depend on what other things exist. We are left, in some cases, in a state of having to resolve the issue one way or the other but the only way of doing this is to specify the criteria we are using. If all we are interested in is Horace being the thing with which we have mixed our labour, then we resolve it one way. If the original Horace was an antique and we are interested in the original parts, we may resolve it the other. The fact that there may only be one candidate for being Horace makes life easier for us but it still remains the case that whether or not we have Horace before us is not a matter entirely resolved by considering the motorcycle in itself. It depends on the existence of other things.

In this chapter, we have been investigating the nature of existence and arriving at what some might take to be surprising conclusions. Much of the discussion has focused on the existentialist approach, which we first encountered when discussing 'existential freedom' in the chapter on the meaning of life. It is now time to pick up on the theme of freedom and broaden it to include the questions concerning our political freedom: why should I be made to wear a helmet if I don't want to, why can't I speed and what grounds are there for punishing me if I break such laws?

Image 3. New Zealander Burt Munro set the land-speed world record at Utah's Bonneville Salt Flats in 1967 on a 1920 Indian, as portrayed in *The World's Fastest Indian* (2005)

Third Gear

Full speed ahead – or riding too fast without a helmet

Traffic Policeman: Do you know how fast you were going out there?

Burt Munro: Yeah, about 150, 160mph.

Traffic Policeman: Yeah ... that sounds ... about right.

The World's Fastest Indian (2005)

There's nothing like firing up the motorcycle on a warm summer's evening and disappearing down some country lanes with nothing but the orange glow of the sun on the horizon and a cool breeze to keep you company. You can go where you like. You can return at any time. Motorcycling, for many, is the ultimate expression of freedom. Or, at least, there is a certain experience we have while riding that many associate with freedom and which cannot be got from driving a car, going by train or walking.[1]

On further reflection, it is not clear why we associate that experience with freedom. We can, after all, go for a walk wherever we like and return at any time. It may be that the freedom we are talking about is of the *existential* sort mentioned in the chapter on the meaning of life, since riding is a 'hands-on', active pursuit, where mistakes can be easy to make and have high costs, in the way car driving, train travelling and walking do not – at least, not as much. It seems much more likely that this is the sort of freedom we mean, since in terms of *political* freedoms, motorcyclists are *less* free than some in certain respects. The state, for instance, does not impose a limit on the speed at which we walk, nor does it require us to wear a helmet when we do so. Then again, motorcycles give us the freedom to go at 70mph in a way walking doesn't; and if we were able to walk that quickly, we may well have been required to wear a helmet. Nevertheless, motorcyclists do have limits imposed on their freedom. Or rather, it is better to say that motorcyclists have the *freedom* to go as fast as their motorcycles can carry them but they are not at *liberty* to do so: they *can* go that fast (it is physically possible) but they *may* not go that fast (it is not permissible). The question is whether there is

[1] Note that we have to say that we *associate* this feeling with freedom rather than say it is an experience *of* freedom, since freedom itself does not *feel like* anything. To see this, suppose you have been locked in a cell for a week. On one of the nights, unbeknownst to you, the door was left unlocked. Had freedom felt like anything, you could have known which night it was, due to that feeling. But since you wouldn't have known from any feeling, freedom does not feel like anything. As Fred Feldman (2006) points out, we shouldn't mistake a feeling of freedom for the feeling of excitement and exhilaration that we get from riding.

any clear justification for imposing such restrictions. There will be many reasons put forward for placing restrictions on our motorcycling activities but many argue that they fall short of justification. In this chapter, we need to ask two questions: first, on what grounds should we allow the state to require that I do not speed and that I wear a helmet; and second, what, if any, should be the legitimate punishment if I violate those restrictions? Any answer to the first question will have a bearing on the second; so we should begin with the first. However, since some of the reasons put forward for restricting speed are different from reasons for requiring helmets to be worn, let's tackle these issues separately.

THE NEED FOR SPEED

Life may begin at thirty but it doesn't get really interesting until 150. If this is true, what is the justification for restricting the speeds at which we may ride? In a famous statement of the so-called 'Harm Principle', the English philosopher John Stuart Mill (1806–1873) writes:

> The only purpose for which power can be rightfully exercised over any member of a civilised community, against his will, is to prevent harm to others. His own good, either physical or moral, is not a sufficient warrant. He cannot rightfully be compelled to do or forbear because it will be better for him to do so, because it will make him happier, because, in the opinion of others, to do so would be wise or even right.

> (Mill 1859: 223–4)

It is clear, if we follow this principle, that the only justification for speeding restrictions is to prevent harm to others. But in what sense does speeding harm anyone? Speeding is speeding and there is nothing intrinsically harmful in that. Of course, it's hitting people that counts and if you hit them at high speed, it's not going to be pretty for either party.[2] Speeding, although not a harm in itself, can be a contributing factor in harm to others. Speed can be cited as a factor in the causal chains leading to crashes but, mostly, it contributes by magnifying the consequences of unsafe riding rather than in being unsafe in itself. Speeding riders have less time to react to changing conditions, as do other road users in their path; speeding does not mix well with poor road, weather and lighting conditions or with motorcycles not fit for their job. Even if riders are fully confident of their own abilities and that of their motorcycles, it's not possible to guarantee that the rest of the world won't stuff things up. Once, while I was out for a ride in the country, I turned a fairly sharp corner only to be greeted by the world's stupidest bird, a pheasant. Not being that bright, it flew towards me rather than away and since I was leaning, I didn't want to grab a handful of brake. Sitting the bike upright to avoid being hit in the face, I was forced onto the grass verge, where I had to ride into a ditch, onto a field and then back safely onto the road. I tell this story to friends with pride, since it is an illustration of a situation where, if you don't panic and remain in control, you can find ways of not coming off the bike. But circumstances might have been different. I wasn't going

---

[2] Best estimates for collision involving cars suggest that five per cent of pedestrians who are struck at 20mph (32km/h) are killed, 45 per cent at 30mph (48km/h) and 85 per cent at 40mph (64km/h) (see Ashton and Mackay (1979)).

particularly quickly, but had I been, things could have been very different. It cannot be denied that lower speeds certainly give the rider more time to react and to react in effective ways – at a greater speed I might have avoided the pheasant, at the cost of being unable to control the bike properly when I flipped it upright or while it was on uneven ground.

The fact that the world might conspire against you, no matter how good a rider you are, is a compelling reason for enforcing strict speed regulations in built-up areas, particularly near schools, where there is an even higher risk of something erratic and fleshy unexpectedly stepping out into the road. Everyone needs to be protected from thoughtless idiots who race around the streets endangering others (the motorcyclists, that is, not the children). They give the responsible riders a very bad name and we should shun them. But where precisely is the harm in speeding, even in front of a school, when you don't hit someone? What should you be punished for? It is not like so-called 'inchoate' offences, such as attempted murder, where there need be no actual harm done, yet the person is still prosecuted. It is not as if speeding riders intend to hit something but fail to do so on some occasions. Maybe we should see it more as a case of being justifiably legislated against not because of any actual harm done but because of the high *risk* of bringing about a highly undesirable outcome. This, to some, may not sound quite right. If I were to suggest that someone should be punished even though they haven't harmed anyone, many people would object. Yet this is what legislating on the basis of risk seems to amount to. But, as we saw in the chapter on death, there are different ways in which we can understand the notion of harm. Those queasy about the idea of punishing someone when they have not harmed anyone may nevertheless say that speeding *is* a direct harm in itself, since it is in the interests of everyone not to be subject to such a risk and so speeding, whether or not it actually brings about a death or other undesirable outcome, violates that particular interest. Either way, this seems to me to be a compelling argument against speeding in built-up areas.[3]

However, it is much less compelling in the case of motorway riding, especially lone motorway riding. Despite higher speeds, motorways are the safest roads per-mile-travelled.[4] To appreciate the reason why, consider the research carried out by Hans Joksch (1993). He found that impact speed was the most important factor determining the risk of death of the occupant of a car in a collision and that the risk of death varied according to the 'rule of thumb' equation:

$$\text{risk of death} = \left(\frac{\text{impact speed (mph)}}{71 \text{ (mph)}}\right)^4$$

If you were to tell your friends this – that the risk of death is the impact speed divided by 71 and raised to the power four – they might think you were winding them up. However, this equation was derived from a number of actual collisions and is a good summary of what was discovered about those crashes. To use some examples: an impact speed of 60mph (97km/h) gives the risk of death as (60/71) squared and then squared again, which is approximately 50 per cent. (The impact speed is

---

[3] The same can be said about riding an unroadworthy vehicle or while under the influence of drugs or alcohol.

[4] Source: International Road Traffic and Accident Database (IRTAD).

derived from speed before impact minus speed after.) Similarly, if you travel at 30mph (48km/h) before the collision and come to a stop after the collision, the impact speed is 30mph (48km/h) and so the risk of death is $(30/71)^4$, which is around three per cent.

This gives some insight into why motorways are relatively safe, despite the high average speed of vehicles on them, since what matters is not so much the speed you are travelling but the speed of the vehicles relative to everything else on the motorway. First, there is effectively no oncoming traffic on a motorway; the risk of high-speed collisions is therefore reduced. Second, slow-moving vehicles are also prohibited, which means less speed variation on each side of the motorway, reducing the impact speed of vehicles travelling in the same direction. Third, there are far fewer roadside obstacles, and pedestrians are restricted from wandering onto motorways. Fourth, no traffic crosses motorways, reducing the risk of side-impact collisions (which, on cars, is the most vulnerable area, and which, on humans, lead to the most serious brain injuries). A different story must be told about the survival of motorcyclists in such collisions but the point is that we (as motorcyclists) are interested in the harm done *to others* when we travel at high speeds, not what harm is done to us, since, according to Mill's Harm Principle above, harm done to others is the only basis on which the state can legitimately legislate against certain actions.

Many of the risks associated with riding in built-up areas do not apply to motorway riding (and to a certain extent some country roads), so the same arguments cannot be so easily used to justify legislation against speeding. However, not all risks are ruled out: road débris, broken-down vehicles, stupid pheasants and so on remain. And it isn't all about risk; it is also about the costs of what could go wrong. Sometimes the costs are so great that even a small risk of them happening rules out allowing certain actions. A pile-up on the motorway, however unlikely, is enough to create extra-cautious legislation. Nevertheless, on a clear stretch of road on a nice day, it is very difficult to see what harm has been done to others. It seems to me that there is little justification for punishment under these circumstances, apart from a rather weak one concerning the need to apply the law consistently. It is not clear that anyone who goes for a blast on a stretch of empty road would even consider doing it under circumstances dangerous to others.

There are, however, two potential qualifications to the view that the lone motorcyclist does no harm. First, they might have dependents (a partner, children, elderly parents) who would suffer both emotional and financial harm if anything serious happened. It is not clear, however, whether the law should have any say in this matter. What else would they prohibit? Where would it stop? Would we, on pain of punishment, be required to exercise and eat healthily? If so, how much time should one serve for eating biscuits in front of the TV? And with some punishments (fines, prison) the dependents suffer as well. Furthermore, this response says nothing about the lone motorcyclist who has no dependents. It might be argued that nobody lives in isolation and we all suffer the consequences of crashes: taxpayers must foot the bill for the emergency services and hospital care, and others in the motorcyclist's insurance pool will suffer as premiums increase. But would we rather live in a society where no one had liberty but where taxpayers saved a little bit of money, or in one where we are willing to pay the cost for the greater benefit of having the liberty to live our own lives? If we were to adopt this 'public charge' argument for placing restrictions on our liberty, very few activities would be left unregulated. The second potential qualification concerns the environment. Although (perhaps surprisingly) motorway driving offers better fuel economy despite the higher average speeds, since they facilitate better traffic flow, higher speeds mean higher fuel consumption and this is bad for the environment. We will have to wait until we discuss the environment in a later chapter to see what should be said about motorcycling and the environment.

Whatever we decide about the lone motorcyclist, it is a feature of democracy that laws are only legitimate when they have the consent of those who are subject to them. It is important that laws have this basis. Consent is, in the main, expressed through having free, fair and regular elections, but since we vote for political parties' package deals rather than single issues, it may be that the only political party offering what you want on a particular issue is so dreadful overall that you don't vote them into government (as is currently the case with the UK Conservative Party). It is evident to anyone who rides on the motorway, at least in the UK, that many people travel faster than the 70mph (113km/h) speed limit, because they feel that 70mph is too slow, especially given the vehicles they use. This has largely come about because the speed limits for UK motorways have not taken account of advances in vehicle design. The speed limit of 70mph (113km/h) first suggested in 1965 (and made permanent in 1967) may well have been appropriate then and for a few subsequent years but there is a case for increasing it to at least 80mph (129km/h) for modern vehicles. According to AASHTO (1994):

> Experience has ... shown that speed limits set arbitrarily below the reasonable and prudent speed perceived by the public are difficult to enforce, produce non-compliance, encourage disrespect for the law, create unnecessary antagonism toward law enforcement officers and divert traffic to lesser routes.

There is, then, an argument for increasing the speed limit, based on the idea of what a successful law is, despite our not electing into power a political party that endorses such an increase. However, this is merely an argument for changing what the speed limit is, not for saying that speed limits are not justified, since, apart from the lone rider on the motorway, it seems they are.

These arguments were all based on the harm done to others but the legitimacy of compulsory helmet laws must have a different basis. Unlike speeding, where no appeal has to be made to protecting the individual rider from themselves, helmet laws rely on it.

SHOULD WE BIN THE LID FOR A BREATH OF FRESH HAIR?

My impression, which could be wrong, is that your attitude towards helmets depends on where you come from and what sort of motorcycle you ride. For instance, it seems that American Harley riders are much more against helmets than British riders of high performance motorcycles. Given its emphasis in their constitution, it may be that the American rider is sensitised to the slightest whiff of an infringement on their liberty, whether or not it is good for them, whereas the British tend to be much more pragmatic: why fight the law when it is clearly sensible to wear a helmet, both for safety and for protection against cold wind and rain, deafening engine and air noise and being pelted by flies and road débris. For me, you can forget the wind blowing through your long straggly hair and awful beard (the classic Harley look): helmets are an opportunity radically to enhance your style and heighten the sense of occasion, by immersing yourself in the ritual of dressing for the ride and strapping on a lid. I wouldn't stop wearing a helmet even if it were allowed. Nevertheless, no matter what I take to be the advantages of wearing a helmet, is it a matter for the state to require that those who do not want to wear them do, and on pain of punishment if they don't?

Is it ever right to do good to others against their wishes? There are clear cases where we think it is: we might force children to brush their teeth and tidy their rooms. But imagine if someone forced *you* to brush *your* teeth and tidy *your* room. Most of us would think that person was stepping over the line; treating you like a child, treating you 'paternalistically'. The case of helmet laws is taken, by some, to be of the same kind; where the claim that to wear a helmet is in your best interest (in the judgement of someone who claims to know better, like a parent knows best for the child), so whether or not you want to wear one, you should – indeed, you *must*. What is in your best interests is assumed to be more important than your liberty. This is taken as illegitimate and offensive by those who do not want to wear helmets. They would claim that paternalism is consistent with Mill's Harm Principle when applied to children or the insane, but for sane, informed adults they see no justification for the requirement to wear a helmet. This sentiment will strike a chord with many but we need to discuss the various ingredients of the position and the ethical framework in which they are couched to see whether or not this kind of paternalistic requirement to wear a helmet is justified.

Mill's Harm Principle states that certain acts should only be prohibited if they harm others who haven't consented to the harm. One way in which we might try to justify legislation is by arguing that the act is plain immoral and society needs protecting from it. This was a view that Judge Sir James Fitzjames Stephen (1829–1894) put forward in his attack on Mill. The debate was re-ignited in an exchange between Judge Lord Devlin (1905–1992) and the legal philosopher H. L. A. Hart (1907–1992), in response to the 1957 Wolfenden Report on Homosexual Offences and Prostitution, which led to the legalisation of homosexuality under the Sexual Offences Act 1967. The Wolfenden Report claimed that 'private immorality' was no business of the criminal law; Devlin disagreed, asserting that, whether or not people were right to think the act immoral, a perceived transgression of a society's core values would lead to a breakdown of that society, so that society can legitimately legislate to stop the act in order to preserve itself.[5]

Whatever we think about that thorny issue, nobody can claim that not wearing a helmet has the status of being an immoral act in itself. Unlike the case where someone wears *nothing but* a helmet, nobody will find it remotely offensive. We cannot argue that these people will ride around flaunting

[5] See Devlin (1965) and Hart's (1963) disagreement.

their naked heads to all and sundry, corrupting the young and encouraging them to 'come out' of the helmet to lead an equally debauched and degrading lifestyle. There's simply nothing to be corrupted by. Not wearing a helmet just isn't one of those kinds of cases.

Let us discuss instead whether it is plausible to think that those adults against helmet laws can be said to be well-informed, since if they are not, there is an argument for not taking the Harm Principle to be applicable and for making them wear a helmet. There is a relatively clear quantitative evaluation that can be made for wearing helmets. We can collect data on the numbers and types of motorcycle accidents involving those wearing and not wearing helmets, including the number of people who died and the number who survived and the types of injuries they sustained. Based on the results of theoretical tests, we could then make an assessment of what would have happened had those people not been wearing a helmet in these conditions, and so on. Studies in the US show that, under universal helmet laws, most states experienced twenty to forty per cent lower fatality rates than during periods without laws or with limited laws, and that helmets are thirty-six per cent effective in preventing death and sixty-five per cent effective in preventing brain injuries.[6]

Given a well-conducted statistical study, this kind of assessment of the advantages of wearing helmets is a factual matter and, as a factual matter, it seems that the arguments are in favour of wearing helmets – that is, if you'd prefer not to be seriously injured or killed on the relatively rare occasions you find

[6] Source: Preusser Research Group Inc. September 2000.

yourself in an accident.[7] Is it ignorance of such statistics that prevents people from making an informed choice about wearing helmets? If those who object to helmet laws are ignorant of the risks, they cannot appeal to the Harm Principle. But could anyone who understands the statistics still want not to wear a helmet? I think the only answer is that some would and some wouldn't. There are at least three different kinds of response from those who would still not wear a helmet: (a) wishful thinking; (b) counter-evidence, and (c) acceptance. Plenty of people adopt (a) and think it wouldn't happen to them. This is a flaw: to use the terminology from earlier in the book, it seems to me to be a rather inauthentic way to be; you cannot ignore what you need to face up to, namely, the real possibility of your own death. One cure to this kind of ignorance is to survive a rather minor accident and then extrapolate.[8] Surviving an accident might encourage you to think you'll always be lucky but what I mean is that, once you appreciate how easily accidents happen, or that it hurts enough when someone rubs their knuckles into your arm (try it!), or you crack your head on a door frame, you can more easily imagine how bad it feels to

[7] But not that rare: see the statistics at the beginning of the death chapter.

[8] I once rode 240 miles (386km) from my parents' home to Cambridge a couple of days after New Year. Freezing cold and glad to be back home, I turned into my street where I met a road surface covered with ice. I got some way down it, slowing as much as I could without braking, but the inevitable loss of traction occurred as I lightly touched the brakes to stop fully at my house and the motorcycle slid from underneath me and we both ended up horizontal, with it on my leg. This occurred at crawling speed and no damage was done to the bike but, even though I wore full protective clothing, I did limp for a good two weeks. It dawned on me then just how bad it could have been had I met a patch of ice at high speed on the motorway, how lucky I was not to have met such a patch in those conditions in the rest of the 240 miles and how I'll never be riding over this period again.

have your head bounce on and scrape along the road, even at 15mph (24km/h)! Some believe too readily what they see in films like *Torque*, where the characters, wearing neither helmet nor gloves, smile and walk away unscathed from a 200mph (322km/h) crash. Some people have lost their sense of how fragile they are. Some are lucky enough to learn from quite minor mistakes, whereas others never get to learn. As someone once said, 'Everyone crashes. Some get back on. Some don't. Some can't.'

I do think that, as a matter of fact, many are either ignorant of or self-deluded about the risks and costs of not wearing a helmet and, in that regard, they cannot use the argument that they are fully competent to counter the argument that they should be forced to wear a helmet. However, there is still a significant number of people who have taken this into consideration but who still would not wear a helmet. These people fall either into group (b) – those with counter-evidence to the risks or (c) – those who accept the risks as stated.

Those in (b) engage in factual matters. They might argue that deaths and head injuries are offset by the increased risk of more severe neck injuries or they might appeal to the phenomenon known as 'risk compensation', where individuals tend to adjust their behaviour in response to perceived changes in risk. Just as individuals tend to be more cautious when their perception of risk or danger increases, they tend to be less cautious when they feel safer or more protected. It may well be that *if* you have an accident, you are almost always better wearing a helmet, but the probability of being in a crash in the first place may be higher because you feel safer. The weight of this consideration would be very hard to quantify but it is doubtful that it would be weighty enough to make it safer not to wear a helmet. The point is that the question of whether or not paternalism is justified for those in group (b) rests on getting the facts concerning the safety of helmets straight. Others would say that these factual issues are irrelevant, that whether or not paternalism is justified does not rest on whether the activity is deemed too risky. These people would claim that something more fundamental is at stake, that certain (perhaps non-quantifiable) values have over-riding importance. These people fall into group (c).

Those in group (c) do not dispute the statistics and are well-informed and not self-deluding but, nevertheless, do not want to wear a helmet. What can be said to justify paternalism? We would have to check there wasn't another factor that would in general invalidate the application of the Harm Principle, such as acting under duress. In what ways may motorcyclists feel duress? There is a sense in which they may be forced into making the wrong decision, due to peer pressure. Until relatively recently, people were often laughed at for wearing bicycle helmets and wouldn't wear them because of such ridicule. Imagine there were no motorcycle helmet laws. Would motorcyclists be in the same position? Would it be legitimate to say that if they will be forced either way (by peers or by the state), it is better to force them to make the right decision by using state pressure rather than have them forced by peer pressure to make the wrong decision for relatively trivial reasons? (Speeding is, perhaps, a more familiar case. Aren't we glad for the excuse not to go any faster when we feel the pressure of other road users to push our speed up a little more?) But aside from the fact that it is not real duress, in the sense that, were they not to ride without a helmet, they would suffer any lasting harm from their peers, and we would in any case expect people to have more backbone, it does not address those who are neither ignorant of or self-deluded about the dangers nor feel any coercion from their peers. Why should these people be made to wear helmets against their wishes?

We could question, as we did with the speeding lone motorway rider, whether not wearing a helmet does no harm to non-consenting others, such as dependents and taxpayers. However, this 'public charge' argument is not one to venture unless we are prepared to place restrictions on all our activities. Why stop at restricting riding without a helmet? Why not ban motorcycle riding altogether? Then, we could all travel around on trams, fully automated so we could travel at any speed without crashing. What an awful world that would be, even if it were technologically and economically viable.

If we suppose that laws are justified on the basis of what is good for people, then whether paternalism is justified depends on what we take to be what is good for people and whether paternalism can achieve it. At the level of those factors that can be quantified, such as life expectancy and other health issues, being forced to wear a helmet is good for you. But if we include non-quantifiable aspects, such as being respected as an autonomous individual allowed to make decisions for ourselves, it might be argued that it cannot possibly be good for us *because* it is against our wishes.

An example of someone who holds this kind of position is the philosopher Immanuel Kant (1724–1804). According to his ethical theory, we should treat people as 'ends in themselves'; they are not to be treated as a means to some further end.

According to Kant, all rational people will think this of themselves and, through reflection, will attribute this value to every other rational person. Viewing every rational individual as an end in themselves forms the basis of all our rights and of what sorts of laws restricting our actions are legitimate. Paternalistic legislation takes away the power of adults to make their own decisions. The justification sometimes offered (that it will be good for adults to conform) is to treat adults as *means* to their own good. Paternalism doesn't treat adults as ends in themselves and so Kantians reject its legitimacy, regardless of the consequences of their decision to carry on. If you accept this Kantian framework, there can be no justification for paternalism.

Some do not go so far as to say that no good can possibly be done to others against their wishes but rather that although it *is* possible to do good, it is outweighed by the bad. Suppose that we take autonomy as one of our values but that its exercise on any particular occasion is not taken to have over-riding weight attached. A reasonable-sounding justification for paternalism can then be made, even if we place autonomy high on our scale of things to value, for it may well be better to limit autonomy in the 'short term' to gain greater autonomy in the 'long term'. For the short-term advantage of not wearing a helmet in sunny weather or the convenience of not having to put on a helmet when our destination is close by, we may be jeopardising our ability to realise our long-term goals due to being paralysed, having brain damage or being dead (all of which, to varying degrees, limit autonomy).

The problem that some have is that the state is legislating against what might be one of our short-term goals, to advance what they presume to be in our long-term interests, and that one is of greater value than the other. Most people know their own minds better than any government official and it is presumptuous to assume what people do want in the long term. (Of course, what people *want* and what is in their *interest* are sometimes different but this just heightens the worry that there could be increasingly intrusive legislation imposed on unwilling people in the name of giving them what they should 'really' want if they were rational.) The argument against paternalism rests on whether governments are in the best position to decide what is in someone's interests, such that it outweighs what can be achieved by the individual's decisions: what we have been calling the 'short-term' benefits of not wearing a helmet on a sunny day may be of such importance to you that a lifetime in the knowledge that you have done such a thing is worth a lifetime in a wheelchair. So long as the individual is well-informed, is not using invalid reasoning and is not unreasonably discounting future benefits against present ones, there seems little justification for forcing them to do what they don't want to do. Nevertheless, others might not be so reflective or omniscient about their interests, in which case we should have no objection to such laws if, on balance, they do us good.

However, it is one thing to question whether someone is justified in forcing you to do something and quite another whether you should do it. For me, even if it were legally permissible not to wear a helmet, I think that I should, in a prudential sense, wear one. My preferences are such that the advantages of not wearing a helmet on a sunny day are not worth even the risk of facial disfigurement, let alone a serious brain injury. But the advantages of riding a motorcycle *itself* certainly are worth the risks and I'd fight against any law that tried to tell me that it was in my long-term interests not to ride and, therefore, that I can't.

We have found some considerations that are relevant to deciding whether certain laws are justified, but if these laws are to be enforced, there will have to be consequences for those who break them. We need next to discuss what the appropriate punishment should be. As we shall see, this is far from clear.

PUNISHMENT

Speeding, causing death by reckless driving, not wearing a helmet, having an non-roadworthy vehicle, parking in prohibited areas, not having tax or insurance, and so on, are all punishable offences, but what is the justification for punishing those who break the law? How do we decide the appropriate severity of the punishment? The offences above range from mere road traffic offences, punished by fines and penalty points on the driving licence, to crimes, punished by imprisonment and bans on riding. Why would it be outrageous to imprison someone for parking in a restricted area but to give someone only a couple of penalty points on their licence for causing death by reckless driving?

There are, broadly, two rival ways we could justify punishment. The first stems from *consequentialist* considerations. Consequentialists justify an action by looking at its consequences, for instance the amount of pleasure it promotes and suffering it reduces. For a consequentialist, the pay-offs of punishing someone should be worth the costs. Since punishment involves the suffering of the person punished, for it to be justified, it must lead either to an overall increase in what is good or a reduction in what is bad. The obvious way this could happen is if the punishment *prevents* the individual from committing more crimes, or *reforms* them, or acts as a *deterrent*, so that the harm of the punishment to the offender is outweighed by the good consequence of a reduction in crime.

The other view of punishment stems from the idea of *retribution*. This is not quite the same concept as revenge, for the concept of revenge does not necessarily incorporate any idea of *justice* or *proportionate* measures. Someone who is justifiably embarrassed in front of friends, family and colleagues may take revenge on the person who caused the embarrassment by ruining their career and driving them into an early grave. These measures go somewhat beyond retribution, both because they were a reaction to an act which was justified and because they were disproportionate to the harm done. Retribution relies on the notion that those who do wrong (and *only* those who do wrong) *deserve* to suffer. Unlike consequentialists, retributivists claim that the suffering is justified by the fact that the perpetrator deserved it, not by the fact that the suffering will have beneficial consequences.

The consequentialist justification has been subject to a number of challenges. For instance, if what matters is the deterrence of certain crimes, it would sanction the punishment of a person (perhaps a person with a high profile, who it could be widely believed was involved) whether or not that person actually perpetrated the crime. Defenders of the view might respond that this would not be allowed because, if it were discovered that this had happened, it would undermine the public's confidence in the justice system. This is a rather weak response, since it doesn't really get to the heart of the issue. The whole problem stems from our sense that punishment should incorporate the notion of *desert* – that is, after all, why the public's confidence in the justice system would be undermined – and so punishment in these circumstances would be wrong, even if nobody discovered that innocent people had suffered for the sake of beneficial results for others.

Another way in which consequentialism may allow for the punishment of those who haven't actually committed any offence is in punishing those we think are more likely to commit them. Although this may prevent certain people committing offences, it may also include those who wouldn't actually have gone on to commit them, and even if it did stop those who would have gone on to commit an offence, they have still been punished for something they didn't do.

In both these cases we can argue against punishing the innocent by appealing to the rights of each individual to be free unless they have harmed unconsenting others. This need not be seen as some kind of constraint added on to a consequentialist theory but rather, as Mill thought, we could see it as having a consequentialist justification in itself. That is, liberties and other rights need not be seen as some kind of 'fundamental human rights' but as justified, if at all, because of the overall benefits they bring. If consequentialists can show that the benefits of having such rights outweigh the benefits of punishing the innocent, then punishing the innocent is indeed unjustified.

Consequentialism has also been attacked for allowing disproportionate punishments. Severe punishments for petty but widespread crimes may have beneficial overall results. Not many sensible people (who weren't desperate) would shoplift if they knew their capture would lead to their hands being cut off, but this seems like an unjust punishment for someone who takes a loaf of bread. They are, in effect, paying for the crime of every other shoplifter, but why should they be responsible for what other people do? In response, a consequentialist could argue that a disproportionate punishment may lead to a far from beneficial situation overall: someone who knows their hands will be cut off may well be more inclined to do whatever they need to do to escape capture, leading to much more violent crimes, and so on. Punishment, consequentialists hope, will regulate itself and converge to a proportionate punishment.

The last feature to mention of the consequentialist approach to punishment is that it does not give due respect to the free choice of individuals. In emphasising the notions of prevention, deterrence and reform, individuals are effectively being manipulated into certain forms of behaviour, rather than as being given free rein to determine their own course of action and suffer whatever consequences they deserve. Deterrence, unlike retribution, does not treat individuals as an end, since it uses them as a means to stopping others from committing crimes (as with shoplifters having their hands cut off).

The retributive theory seems better on all these counts, since it incorporates the notions of just and proportionate measures, but it encounters a problem when trying to say what punishment is *for*. It is not, primarily, for reducing crime; it is primarily used because the individual *deserves* it. What does this mean?

Is it redressing a balance? Has the offender attained an unfair advantage over others who conform to the law? Law-abiding citizens accept the burdens imposed by living in a secure state; wrongdoers just accept the benefits – they are protected by the laws but they themselves break them. The wrongness of their offence is in taking an unfair advantage. However, murder is committed against an individual and is punished because of it, not because the murderer had an unfair advantage. What sort of advantage is gained? Do others really feel restrained by the law in this way? Would they murder if it weren't illegal? Nevertheless, this might be the rationale for punishing other offences, such as not having any road tax. It is clear what advantage is had here but it is hard to see what advantage is taken in not wearing a helmet.

What principles underlie the punishing of speeding and of not wearing a helmet? In the case of most speeding, we have seen that there is a clear justification for such laws, based on the Harm Principle. We need not see this as being different from punishing any other violation of a non-paternalistic law. However, a different story must be told in the case of helmets. Surely punishment can't be for retributive reasons, since it isn't clear that there is any untoward behaviour in the first place and even if there is harm, it seems odd for the state to punish *you* for harms done to *you* (whether or not they were done *by* you). In what sense do you deserve that punishment, any more than a victim of any offence deserves punishment? Retribution cannot be the underlying reason for punishment here. Should it be rehabilitation, reform or deterrence? If deterrence, the punishment should be a penalty, so people are deterred but, if it is to be rehabilitative, it should also be compulsory classes on the dangers of not wearing a helmet. The problem is that, although there will be many riders who would change their ways after being made aware of the statistics or looking at photos of accident scenes, there will be riders who would still say that they understand all that and yet still want to ride without a helmet. These riders would have to have had their mind changed about riding without a helmet before the punishment could have been said to be effective. In not changing their minds after attending such classes, should they be given higher fines and exposed to more gruesome photos? If that doesn't work, should they be taken to an accident scene to look at the state of a mangled rider who hadn't worn a helmet? Should they then be sent to prison? All this because they have a different set of preferences to other people; this is hard to swallow. It is particularly hard to see what punishment would be justified for not wearing a helmet, because it is difficult to see what harm has been done. So, let us assume that it is justified and see whether there is a satisfactory account of punishment in general.

Since, in general, neither the consequentialist nor the retributive view work by themselves, perhaps we need to mix the best aspects of both. Hart (1968) suggests that we solve the retributivist's problem of specifying what punishment is for by appealing to the consequentialist answer – it is to reduce crime through prevention, deterrence or reform – but to solve the consequentialist's problem with unjust treatment by appeal to the retributivist answer – only the guilty may be punished and only in proportion to the severity of the crime.

We still have a problem in specifying what it is to be proportionate. Is it an eye for an eye? Some seem to think that this is straightforward in the case of murder, but what if you murdered someone out of mercy? How could you be mercifully killed in return? This position makes even less sense in the cases of speeding and of not wearing a helmet. 'An eye for an eye' is not all well and good but 'a not-wearing-a-helmet for a not-wearing-a-helmet' or 'a speeding for a speeding' are even worse: they're nonsense. To say that the punishment must be 'proportionate' cannot, in all cases, mean that it must resemble the offence. Nevertheless, there may be other ways in which we can represent proportion other than through it resembling the offence, such as through the length of prison sentences or size of fine. Fines and prison sentences do deter and may be all that is required to justify their appropriateness for excessive speeding.

But there is a puzzle surrounding the use of such punishment that is particularly relevant to people, such as motorcyclists, who are usually punished by fines. We can see this by asking whether it is morally legitimate for someone voluntarily to suffer a punishment meant for someone else. Most of the time, it isn't. My mother should not be able to go to prison for my crime of murder to save me from having to go; neither should we allow rich people to hire others to take their punishment for them. Innocent people should not take the punishment. If they endured the whole stretch in prison and we found out that such a deal had taken place between the wealthy guilty party and person who was paid to take the rap, we would still feel that the guilty person had to have the punishment he thought he'd been able to buy himself out of.

But as some have pointed out (for example, Lewis 1997), it seems we are inconsistent. Any punishment involving fines is subject to this kind of substitution yet we do not think there is anything wrong in someone paying another's fines or giving money to someone who has paid a fine. This punishment, then, will not always serve as a deterrent. It might, in the case of a poor family having to pay a fine, in shaming the guilty person into a better way of life, but not if the fine is paid by a wealthy person (for example, a crime boss). It might depend on the rationalisation for the fine. If it were compensation, it wouldn't matter who paid it. But fines are not handed over to victims (if there are any). So, compensation isn't the reason for the fine (unless it's in a vague sense in which the community is the victim). Given that we cannot keep track of where the money has come from, to make sure that it is the perpetrator of the crime who has paid the fine rather than someone else, should we abandon fines as punishments and send people to prison instead? Is it not inconsistent to allow someone to pay another's fine but not to go to prison for them? If not, what grounds are there for differentiating?

Our choice, however, need not be between prison or a fine, so we can perhaps avoid the puzzle over appropriate punishment. The answer lies in more inventive and useful ways of punishing people – indeed, what is required as an appropriate measure may well be so different from traditional measures that we should stop calling it 'punishment'. If our primary aim in punishing someone is to reduce offences by reforming them, a necessary element of the punishment must be to re-educate. It wouldn't matter who paid for that, so long as the perpetrator took the course. This would not be the 'soft' option because, combined with a points system, where more points are added to the licence after each offence, those who continued to break the rules would suffer loss without having to be imprisoned or fined – they'd be banned from riding. Only by identifying where the harm is in a particular offence can we possibly make sense of the idea of the punishment fitting the offence and this will require much more inventive responses to offences than generic prison sentences and fines.

Image 4. An argument for leathers? Uma Thurman in *Kill Bill: Vol. I* (2003)

Fourth Gear

40
160
180
200

Saving your bacon: the rights and wrongs of wearing leather

Lisa: Do we have any food that wasn't brutally slaughtered?
Homer: Well, I think the veal died of loneliness.

The Simpsons

I have talked so far about the rights of humans and the value of their lives. It is now time to consider the rights of animals and the value of their lives. Leathers are the clothing of choice for most serious motorcyclists, both for safety and style. This use of animals is hardly ever questioned, at least by motorcyclists but can it be justified? Some argue it can because, unlike humans, animals lack language, abstract reasoning and conceptual abilities and perhaps even any real capacity to experience pain. So, since they are of a 'lower' status than humans, they do not deserve our moral consideration. Others think that such 'higher' faculties as linguistic and conceptual ability are irrelevant to assessing the moral status of animals and how they can legitimately be treated. As we shall see, the truth lies somewhere between these two extremes. Whether it is legitimate for motorcyclists to use animals for their skins will be seen to depend on a number of factors.

A LITTLE HISTORY[1]

Serious concern for the welfare of animals is nothing new. The Ancient Greek philosopher and mathematician Pythagoras (c. 570–c. 497 BCE) was, famously, vegetarian. However, his reason arose from his view that the souls of dead men migrate to animals, so was only based on concern for animals in so far as they have this connection to humans. I don't know how many people have converted to vegetarianism because of serious worries that deceased relatives may be on the dinner table but none of the arguments I shall consider will rest on it.[2]

A few centuries after Pythagoras, the Roman Plutarch (c. 45–c.120 CE) was apparently the first to argue, in his *Moralia*, that using any sentient creature for human pleasure was wrong, independently of any belief in the transmigration of souls. Some later medieval Christian writers also condemned cruelty

---

[1] See Peter Singer (1975: chapter 5) for more details; but a more rigorous account can be found in Sorabji (1993).

[2] If some reports are to be believed, Pythagoras was a strange chap. He founded a religion, which, according to Burnet (1892), among other things banned the eating of beans and specified that one must not allow swallows to share one's roof. But just how much dafter this is than what you can find in other religions, I wouldn't be prepared to say.

to animals, St Neot (?–c. 870) being one; famed for his 'strange ways' with birds and animals, he even sabotaged hunts, despite being only four feet tall. St Francis of Assisi (c.1181– 1226) is also renowned for the love he extended to all animals, although some don't take this too seriously, since he thought much the same about rocks. And Francis' all-encompassing feelings of compassion were not quite overwhelming enough to stop him from eating the objects of his affection (the animals, that is, not the rocks).

Leonardo da Vinci (1452–1519) was probably the most famous vegetarian of the Renaissance while Michel de Montaigne (1533–1592) in his essay 'On Cruelty' argued that cruelty to animals was wrong, independent of any worry that it might lead to cruelty to humans (although the contemporary philosopher Daniel Dennett accuses de Montaigne of being 'a gullible romantic of breathtaking ignorance, eager to take the most fanciful folktales of animal mentality at face value and not at all interested in *finding out* ... how animals actually work' (Dennett 1995)). Their writings express a clear interest in animal welfare, albeit an interest swimming against the tide of this time, for the dominant humanist movement had given humans a central place in the universe, pushing the interests of animals to the side.

Around this time, empirical science as we understand it started to flourish and many reports exist of dissections performed on live animals in the name of science. Not that this was necessarily thought to be cruel. For instance, the philosopher and true Renaissance man René Descartes, who we met in our discussion of scepticism about the external world, argued that animals were mere automata. He believed that the world worked in a mechanical way; a fruitful framework which enabled him to develop all sorts of ingenious mathematical and physical methods. But to reconcile this mechanical outlook of the world and everything in it with a concept of human beings as free creatures, he argued that humans also have a non-physical aspect, which is not subject to the mechanical laws which govern physical bodies. Descartes formulated arguments for taking the non-physical substance to be the seat of consciousness, thought and feeling but animals were not deemed to have such a non-physical aspect and, consequently, were not considered to be capable of feeling pain. As a result, Descartes himself became the evil demon, not by subjecting humans to systematic error but by subjecting animals to systematic abuse, through vivisection and needless cruelty.

At least, that's the simple story that is regularly told about Descartes' relationship with animals (see Singer 1975: 201, for instance). The correct assessment of his views is much more complex. Despite now having a bad reputation for inflicting cruelty on animals in the name of science, there is no evidence to suggest that Descartes ever performed any operations on animals or thought we were free to use them as we saw fit. As the Descartes scholar John Cottingham explains, 'automata' for Descartes probably had its strict Greek meaning of 'self-moving thing', from which it simply cannot be inferred that he meant something which could not feel.[3] Indeed, even though Descartes says explicitly that animals do not think, he also says 'all the things which dogs, horses and monkeys are made to do are merely expressions of their fear, their hope or their joy; and

---

[3] Cottingham (1978); see also Lieber (1988).

consequently, they can do these things without any thought.'[4] In other words, he claims that their inability to think does not rule out their being able to feel fear, hope and joy. As he says, 'I should like to stress that I am talking of thought, not of ... sensation; for ... I deny sensation to no animal, in so far as it depends on a bodily organ.'[5]

This leaves Descartes in an uncomfortable position, reconciling his view that the non-physical aspect of the person, not the physical bodily aspect, is the seat of this mental activity. For Cottingham, this simply means that Descartes had trouble formulating a consistent position, not that he was a sadistic animal abuser. Nevertheless, it seems to me that if Descartes had been consistent, followed through his views on the separateness of the non-physical mind from the physical body and been correct that animals have no mental life, it is hard to see that accusations of cruelty could be made to stick. But since it is not clear whether or not, or to what extent, he did hold such views, and since it is not something which matters for our purposes, we should move on.

A significant advance in the case for the moral consideration of animals can be found in the writings of some of the Enlightenment philosophers of the eighteenth century, much of it in response to the views held by some (or thought to be held by some, as in the case of Descartes), concerning the capacity of animals to feel pain. The Scottish philosopher, David Hume (1711–1776), for instance, thought that we are 'bound by the laws of humanity to give gentle usage to these creatures' (Hume 1751: §III), although he did not think that animals have

[4] J. Cottingham, R. Stoothoff, D. Murdoch and A. Kenny (eds.) (1991: 303).
[5] Ibid., 366.

rights and that their interests could be trumped by those of humans. This attitude was somewhat countered by the other giant of the Enlightenment period, Immanuel Kant, who stated that: 'So far as animals are concerned, we have no direct duties. Animals are not self-conscious and are there merely as a means to an end. That end is man' (Kant, *Lectures on Ethics*: 239–240).

The nineteenth century saw further positive developments in the animal welfare cause, with, in Great Britain, some laws being passed to protect animals against unnecessary cruelty. It was at this time that the forerunner of the Royal Society for the Prevention of Cruelty to Animals (RSPCA) was founded, to see that the laws were enforced. Many of the Bills were ridiculed and rejected and most of those that did get through survived only because they were really based on protecting the rights of humans (such as protecting property rights over animals) rather than directly based on the rights of animals (which was no good for animals not owned by humans or for those with cruel owners). So, although by the nineteenth century some of the grounds for introducing the idea that animals have interests that matter had been cleared, the widespread public concern for how animals can legitimately be treated, with which we are now all so familiar, is a relatively recent phenomenon.

ANIMAL LIBERATION

The examples above are by no means the only examples of writing which can be found in favour of animals having considerable interests, but I think it is fair to say that the so-called 'animal rights movement' really took off and became a substantial and respectable topic of discussion for philosophers after the 1975 publication of *Animal Liberation* by the Australian philosopher, Peter Singer. However, the popular term 'animal rights' is rather misleading. The notion of a right conjures up the idea of it being, in some way, the most basic thing that can be asserted, which does not require any further justification and which trumps any other, less fundamental, claims. It is popular to think, for example, that everyone has a right to life and that this right is a given, which requires no further justifying argument and trumps someone else's desire to detonate bombs in the nearest public building. Many who argue that animals deserve moral consideration – have 'rights' – do not do so on the basis that animals have rights in the sense just sketched: some argue that rights have to be grounded in something more basic; that there should be some more fundamental reason for the right. This approach recognises that there are such things as rights; it just differs in that, whereas the first approach takes rights as a basic notion, the second doesn't.

Singer, for instance, starts his defence from a *utilitarian* perspective, which can be traced back to the eighteenth-century English political philosopher, Jeremy Bentham (1748–1832), who writes:

Nature has placed mankind under the governance of two sovereign masters, *pain* and *pleasure*. It is for them alone to point out what we ought to do, as well as to determine what we shall do. On the one hand the standard of right and wrong, on the other the chain of causes and effects, are fastened to their throne.

(Bentham 1789: Chapter I, paragraph I)

This statement makes two claims, one *descriptive*, the other *prescriptive*. The descriptive claim is that the way that humans are is that they have only two fundamental motivations: to seek pleasure and to avoid pain. The prescriptive claim is that actions are to be judged in terms of their being right or wrong on the basis of whether they contribute to increasing pleasure or pain. The descriptive claim grounds what legislation *could* achieve, given what is taken to be fundamental to human nature and the prescriptive claim grounds what legislation *should* aim to achieve; the maximising of pleasure and the minimising of pain. One of Bentham's projects was to re-cast existing legislation, where a clear and objective justification for it could not always be found, into terms that were clear, objective and fundamental to the concerns of humans. He hoped that justifying legislation in terms of the amount of pain or pleasure that would result from implementing and acting on it would give a clear and objective measure for the rightness or wrongness of an action and ground the conferring of rights.

Bentham saw quite clearly the implications of this for the treatment of animals. In a statement that, quite rightly, has become a classic, he writes:

> The day may come when the rest of the animal creation may acquire those rights which never could have been withholden from them but by the hand of tyranny. The French have already discovered that the blackness of the skin is no reason why a human being should be abandoned without redress to the caprice of a tormentor. It may one day come to be recognised that the number of legs, the villosity of the skin or the termination of the

os sacrum are reasons equally insufficient for abandoning a sensitive being to the same fate. What else is it that should trace the insuperable line? Is it the faculty of reason or perhaps the faculty of discourse? But a full-grown horse or dog is beyond comparisons a more rational, as well as a more conversable animal, than an infant of a day or a week or even a month old. But suppose they were otherwise, what would it avail? The question is not, Can they reason? nor Can they talk? but Can they suffer?

(Bentham 1789: Chapter 17, footnote)

Given Bentham's project to rest morality on the clear foundations afforded by the framework of pain and pleasure, we can understand why he sets aside as irrelevant those features which distinguish humans from animals, such as their linguistic ability and capacity to reason. His claim is that, in so far as animals can feel pain and pleasure, they should be accorded some moral consideration. Pain is pain. If the capacity to feel pain matters in morality, we should no more tolerate pain caused to animals than we should tolerate pain caused to those of a different race or sex. The psychologist Richard Ryder coined the term 'speciesism' for this kind of discrimination and took it seriously enough to refuse to conduct any more experiments on animals. However, most people who are familiar with the term will probably have heard it in connection with Peter Singer's work.

Singer's starting point is the *equal consideration of interests*. Anything which has interests should have those interests taken into account. If only white males had interests, there would be no need to extend any considerations to any other sex or race. But, of course, they're not. It would be illegitimate not to take into consideration the interests of, for example, Asian women *simply because* they're not white males. That would be both racist and sexist. By analogy, to ignore the interests of animals *simply because* they are not of the same species is unacceptable; it is speciesist. This is not to say that animals should be treated *equally* to humans, any more than it follows that men should be treated equally to women. Different individuals have different interests. Dogs do not need to learn how to write, and horses do not require trial by jury, any more than I need a wheelchair or a smear test. Equal consideration of interests respects the needs of those with the interest. It's not in my interest to have my shoes nailed to my feet or for a speculum to be inserted into any of my orifices, but it is if you're a horse or a woman (respectively, that is).

Bringing animals into the equation assumes that animals have interests. Singer states that 'the capacity for suffering and enjoyment is a *prerequisite for having interests at all*, a condition that must be satisfied before we can speak of interests in a meaningful way' (Singer 1975: 7). However, this statement is false. We can easily imagine taking some medication which causes us to lose our capacity to feel pain and pleasure without thereby losing all our interests. In any case, Singer's statement is not quite what is required to ascribe interests to animals. All it says is that the capacity for suffering and enjoyment is a necessary condition for having interests, which is to say that if you have interests then you have the capacity for suffering and enjoyment. But it doesn't follow that if you have the capacity for suffering and enjoyment, then you have interests; that is, that the capacity for suffering and enjoyment is a *sufficient* condition for having interests. But since that is precisely what is required, what we should say is that the capacity for suffering and enjoyment gives humans at least one way in which we can be said to have interests. So, if animals have this capacity, then they have interests.

The question is whether animals have the capacity to suffer and the extent to which they do. It may have seemed obvious to Bentham that whether animals can reason or talk is irrelevant to the moral issue but, as we shall see, the sorts of harms that animals can suffer will, to some extent, depend on what we say about these supposedly irrelevant issues. So, before we can talk meaningfully about animal liberation, we must first discuss animal deliberation.

ANIMAL DELIBERATION

Like many of his predecessors and contemporaries, the Ancient Greek philosopher Aristotle (384–322 BCE) was interested in fundamental philosophical questions concerning the universe and our place in it. He was also interested in empirical matters of fact, which he didn't investigate using pure thought alone but by making careful observations and classifications to develop his theories. He used his empirical findings to construct a theory not just of how humans fit into the scheme of things but also of where animals figure in it.

According to Aristotle, everything in the universe is to be explained in terms of its purpose or proper function. The hierarchy of organisms, from plant life up to humans, together with the view that everything in the universe has a purpose, leads to the view that the purpose of a plant is to nourish an animal and the purpose of an animal is to nourish a human. As a biological theory, this is hard to defend, in the light of Darwin's theory of evolution; interpreted as some kind of theological claim, it is on as shaky foundations as any claim can be. Nevertheless, Aristotle does make interesting observations concerning the differences between humans and animals, which can survive in a modern worldview and, indeed, fit well into the contemporary debate. So we should sketch his view.

According to Aristotle, plants have the capacity to nourish themselves – this is common to all living things, but for plants, this is their *only* capacity. So, each aspect of a plant is explained in terms of how it contributes to the capacity of the plant to nourish itself.[6] However, animals are different from plants, because they are mobile. Thus, the explanation for animals having sense organs is that they facilitate their moving around, which facilitates their ability to nourish themselves.[7] It is this that gives rise to Aristotle's claim that animals can clearly be said to have desires, since a desire for food explains why the animal moves, as does the desire for sex and the desire to avoid pain.[8] For Aristotle, there is no distinction between animals and humans, in so far as they all perceive the world using their sense organs and in so far as they all communicate the pleasures and pains that they feel. But humans are superior to animals, in that they have a capacity to communicate desires of a complexity that, in going beyond the communication of mere sensual desires, far outstrips the capacity of any animal.

However, it is not the degree of complexity of animal desires that distinguishes them from humans. For Aristotle, the

[6] See Aristotle *De Anima* (On the Soul), 416a.
[7] Ibid., 434b.
[8] Ibid., 414b.

difference between animals and humans is not one of degree but of something more fundamental: their lack of *rationality*. To be rational, we must have the capacity to make judgements based on the perceptions of what we take to be the case. But animals, according to Aristotle, lack any concept of the possibility that their perceptions could be false, in which case, they cannot really be said to be making any real judgements, since they cannot help but accept the evidence of their senses.[9] Since it is not within the capacity of the animal to consider alternatives and weigh them against each other, there is no sense in which the animal can be said to be judging anything. Because of their inability to make judgements, Aristotle claims that animals simply do not have beliefs; rather, the experience of animals is much more passive (what he calls 'imagination'): 'The conviction that accompanies all belief is produced by persuasion, a task of reason, and while some of the beasts have imagination, none has reason.'[10]

This, in many ways, is similar to the view of the American philosopher, Donald Davidson (1917–2003). In terms of the complexity of the thoughts which can be communicated, he argues that for the thought to be sufficiently fine-grained, language is required:

The dog, we say, knows that its master is home. But does it know that Mr Smith (who is his master) or that the president of the bank (who is that same master), is home? We have no real idea how to settle or to make sense of, these questions ... [U]nless there is behaviour that can be

[9] Ibid., 427b.
[10] Ibid., 428a.

interpreted as speech, the evidence will not be adequate
to justify the fine distinctions we are used to making in
the attribution of thoughts.

(Davidson 1975: 163)

Davidson goes further in taking this not just to be a question of
our lack of *evidence* for the belief. He argues that, to have a
belief, we must have the *concept* of a belief. However, to have
the concept of a belief we must be part of a community which
uses language, for we are continually *interpreting*, in our language, what other language users say (or inscribe or otherwise
perform). The notion of an interpretation brings with it the difference between what is believed to be the case and what actually is the case. A creature who is not a member of a community
of language users will not come to appreciate the difference
between *believing* something to be true and it *being* true – they
will not appreciate the possibility of being in error. This only
comes, according to Davidson, at the level of interpretation. So,
to have a belief, we must have the concept of a belief, since part
of the concept of a belief is the appreciation of the possibility of
being in error. (As we saw above, this is Aristotle's view that
you cannot have a belief without recognising the possibility of
being in error.) Since, for Davidson, this possibility arises at the
level of interpretation and since animals do not have a language
in which to interpret others, they do not have the concept of
belief and so they do not have beliefs at all. In other words, there
cannot be thought without language (Davidson 1975: 170).

It is not entirely clear that this fully captures our notion of
what it is to have a belief, and why, to ascribe beliefs to them, it
should matter whether the animal has a language. Even if we go

along with Davidson that language is central to the notion of belief, so long as *humans* have a language in which to interpret animal behaviour, it seems quite plausible to say that animals can be ascribed beliefs. Their lack of language just means that they are unable to express a *fine-grainedness* of thought, not that they cannot have thoughts at all. This is not a problem concerning how we can *know* what it is that animals believe; that in some sense we should think of language as just a means of uncovering the complex thoughts that are hidden in the animal's head. The problem arises more from the idea that there are *no* such beliefs when there's no possible way in which they can be expressed; more a consequence of *what it is* to have a belief. Beliefs *make a difference* to how we behave and an obvious way in which we behave differently is to say different things. My linguistic behaviour marks a difference, for example, between my belief that the president of the bank is home and my belief that Mr Smith is not, for I might assert, 'The president of the bank is home', but refuse to assert 'Mr Smith is home'.[11] The question is how animals, without any linguistic resources, can make such distinctions for them to be able to be said to have the different beliefs in the first place.

It seems to me that, even if we assume animals have no language in the way that humans do, it doesn't stop them from expressing themselves adequately in non-linguistic behaviour and doesn't stop us from interpreting that behaviour accordingly. This non-linguistic behaviour may not be sufficient to determine whether they believe that *the president of the bank is home* – it would be implausible to ascribe any such complex

[11] We should not, though, go too far: just having a new or different word does not in itself show that we have a new or different concept of something.

belief – but it wouldn't be implausible to ascribe a belief equivalent to something like *master is home*. After all, the consequences we would expect from having that belief go through: they get excited and only wait at the door just before they expect their master to enter; they don't bark at and bite the person who has walked in but jump up and lick their face; they obey commands, rather than ignore them; they head towards one house rather than another when they have been out for a walk. All this is part of the idea of what it is to have beliefs about masters and homes. Most adult humans also appreciate more sophisticated connotations of these notions, such as legal ownership, but just because our comprehension of the matter is, so to speak, set at a higher resolution than that of a non-language user, we should not conclude that the content of a belief had by an animal with no language is so blurred as to be completely unusable. There is a sufficiently clear boundary around that belief to serve to distinguish it from another. The same goes for desire. If animals want to eat, they'll go where they believe there is food and not elsewhere. If they don't want to eat, they won't bother going to where they believe there is food (unless that is also a place to play, or sleep, or lick their bits, or whatever).

This general approach to beliefs and desires is championed by Daniel Dennett. The fact that it is so practically and theoretically useful to predict, explain and manipulate animal behaviour within a framework wherein we ascribe beliefs and desires to the animals is good enough for us to be able to say that, to all intents and purposes, they have beliefs and desires. Dennett calls the strategy of treating animals as rational agents, whose actions are those they deem most likely to further their desires given their beliefs, the 'intentional stance' (see Dennett 1971; 1987).

This understanding of rationality in terms of applying the notions of belief and desire in accounting for action follows in the footsteps of Hume. Hume defends this method as being:

> ... a species of Analogy, which leads us to expect from any cause the same events, which we have observed to result from similar causes ... The anatomical observations, formed upon one animal, are, by this species of reasoning, extended to all animals ... and any theory, by which we explain the operations of the understanding or ... of the passions in man, will acquire additional authority, if we find, that the same theory is requisite to explain the same phenomena in all other animals.
>
> (Hume 1748: §IX)

So, because the physiology of animals is not that much different from human physiology (in having brain, heart, lungs, nervous system and so on that work in a similar way to those of humans), there are sufficient analogies for us to think that the same approach should be taken towards humans and animals and to think well of an over-arching theory which can be universally applied.

However, there are surely other reasons for ascribing beliefs and desires to certain creatures, even though their physiology is entirely different. In a discussion concerning pain, the American philosopher David Lewis (1941–2001) writes:

> There might be a Martian who sometimes feels pain, just as we do but whose pain differs greatly from ours in its physical realisation. His hydraulic mind contains nothing like our neurons. Rather, there are varying amounts of

fluid in many inflatable cavities and the inflation of any one of these cavities opens some valves and closes others. His mental plumbing pervades most of his body – in fact, all but the heat exchanger inside his head. When you pinch his skin you cause no [events in a brain, in the way that humans have] – he has none – but, rather, you cause the inflation of many smallish cavities in his feet. When theses cavities are inflated, he is in pain. And the effects of his pain are fitting: his thought and activity are disrupted, he groans and writhes, he is strongly motivated to stop you from pinching him and to see to it that you never do again. In short, he feels pain but lacks the bodily states that either are pain or else accompany it in us.

(Lewis 1980)

I think we should agree with Lewis that our concept of pain is robust enough to be employed without hesitation to the Martian. In the presence of certain causes that we would recognise as giving rise to pain in us (pinching), the Martian reacts in the same way as would we (groaning and writhing). Since animals display the same sorts of behaviour in response to similar causes, such states should be classified as painful as well. This typical behaviour, together with the fact that their physiology is closer to ours than that of any Martian described by Lewis, makes overwhelming the case for extending pain states to animals.

It seems to me that we can say the same about beliefs and desires. Humans go to the kitchen when they desire food because that is where they believe the food to be. Martians do the same (only what they would take to be food and where they'd keep it would, no doubt, differ). But if we are so clear, in the Martian case, about employing the notions of belief and desire to explain their behaviour, since animals are much closer to us than any Martian, they surely qualify to have those notions attributed to them.[12]

The question we need to address, in light of this, is whether and to what extent the fact that animals can be said to have sensations, such as pain, as well as (coarse-grained) beliefs and desires, bears on their status in moral matters. We need to consider the sorts of harms to which they can be subject, given their mental life, and we need to address the extent to which they can be considered as 'moral agents'.

WHAT DOES DELIBERATION MATTER?

We have seen that animals can, quite naturally, be said to have beliefs and so, at some level, a capacity to think. What they do not seem to have is the capacity to reflect on their beliefs. To be conscious is, at least, to have beliefs *about* our beliefs;[13] so no animal can be conscious, let alone self-conscious. This claim is highly controversial. There have been many empirical studies claiming that some animals deliberate and reflect on their choices, such as Jane Goodall's famous work with apes (see Goodall 1971), and Allen and Beatrice Gardner's project of teaching American sign language to the chimpanzee Washoe, which, despite its shortcomings, has been used by some to

---

[12] Some things may be so unlike us that we cannot say whether the behaviour can be classified as painful or not. Plants have limited behaviour and completely different physiology. Computers are the same. Kettles even less so.

[13] I believe Armstrong (1968) first suggested this. See also Mellor (1980).

support the view that there is nothing in principle to rule out at least some animals learning a language like our own. Although I see no reason for thinking that no non-human animal could be self-consciousness, let us set these empirical considerations to one side. We should be especially wary of extending the results of empirical research concerning the 'higher' animals to all other animals, since, first, although I don't know whether anyone has tried to teach sign language to cows (although I'd love to see someone try), this is a more relevant case for our purposes, since nobody uses ape-skin to make motorcycle leathers, and, second, if we can argue the case for animals having moral status, without having to show they have consciousness, then establishing whether or not they do have consciousness is an unnecessary diversion. Let us concede, then, for the sake of argument, that animals lack deliberation. How does this stop them from being taken into moral consideration?

We might argue as follows: lions do not worry over the rights and wrongs of killing zebras, so we should not worry over the rights and wrongs of killing lions. There are a couple of things to say about this kind of argument. First, there are many animals on which humans inflict pain and suffering but which do not themselves inflict either. (What has the average pig ever done to anyone?) Yet these sorts of animals are killed in their millions for food and clothing. Appealing to what lions get up to is merely a smokescreen and entirely irrelevant. Second, and more philosophically interesting, we may think that even if lions did deliberate, we might still not hold it to be morally wrong to kill zebras. Lions do not do it merely for fun, nor do they do it for the luxury of having zebra meat: they do it for survival. It may involve suffering but, so far as the lion is concerned, it is far from *unnecessary* suffering. Lions can't grow crops and they can no more eat grass than can we. If they didn't kill, they'd die. Given that their only means of killing the zebra is in a brutal attack involving sharp teeth and powerful jaws, suffering must be involved. But we can't say that it's wrong, not because we should excuse what comes naturally to some animals – what comes naturally is not always right – or because they themselves have no moral code, but rather because if they did have one, this sort of act would not be considered wrong. No moral mode worth considering would prescribe a measure which would render the species extinct in a matter of days. The function of morality is to help make the best of the situations we find ourselves in and to make the right decision, given certain parameters. It wasn't wrong for stone-age humans to hunt animals for their meat and skins – what else could they do to survive? – but it is far from the situation we in the industrialised world are in.

To endorse such a *relativistic* attitude towards morality is not to say that 'anything goes'. It is perfectly consistent to say that killing animals for food and clothing is wrong – *objectively* wrong, if you prefer – in a society like our own but not wrong for those in less comfortable environments or situations. To argue that peasants in Siberia aren't wrong for killing animals for warm fur in the winter has no bearing on how *we* should treat animals. Conversely, if we in Britain decide that we need not kill animals, no matter what Siberians do to animals in Siberia, when they come here there is certainly no need to continue the killing, so they shouldn't. In other words, the kind of relativism I am endorsing does impose constraints on action. We can see this by considering a couple of examples. Suppose that we are betting on Valentino Rossi winning the 2006 MotoGP Championships and that we judge it relative to the evidence that he has won every year since its creation in 2002. Everyone should judge the probability of his winning in 2006 – the so-called 'epistemic' probability – to be quite high. However, if we discover that in 2006 he is planning to race on a 30cc home-made tricycle then, relative to this evidence, everyone should judge the probability to be low. Even though the probabilities are *relative* to evidence, there is a correct way to judge the probability of Rossi winning in each case.[14] (In fact, we now know that he came second, but this in no way invalidates what has been said.)

Or consider a different analogy, this time from physics. The special theory of relativity has the consequence that certain events – such as the event of a parachute opening and the entirely causally unconnected event of a man falling over at a wedding – can be judged to occur at the same time for one person (call her Emily) but not for someone else (call him Felix) who is moving at a constant velocity with respect to Emily. Just because judgements of simultaneity are relative in this sense, it does not follow that the notion of simultaneity is useless or empty, still less does it show that 'anything goes' with respect to judgements of it. The notion of simultaneity remains perfectly meaningful to both Emily and Felix; it's just that they make different judgements regarding it. Further, although it may not make sense to ask, without further qualification, who is right in their judgement of simultaneity, we can say that if Felix were in Emily's position, he would be in error (objectively

---

[14] See Mellor (2005) for more on the philosophy of probability.

wrong, if you like) not to agree with Emily. So there *are* constraints; there is a perfectly clear sense in which we can be right and wrong in our judgements with respect to a given set up.[15]

What goes for judgements of epistemic probability and simultaneity can be applied to judgements of moral rightness and wrongness. It makes no sense to ask whether killing is wrong in the abstract; the question only makes sense in a given context (either implicitly or explicitly specified). Yet, once we've specified the context relative to which the judgement is being made, we can meaningfully determine the rightness or wrongness of it. Neither does it follow, from this kind of relativism, that people be allowed to hide behind common practices and traditions. When considering how to make moral judgements within a particular context, we should not ask what it is that *they* do in that situation based on all *their* background beliefs but what *we* should do in that situation, based on what *we* believe. That is to say, what we shouldn't do is ask, 'If I were irrational or had false beliefs, what would I do?' because that

---

[15] For the full story and a proper discussion of special relativity and its implications see my (2006a) book. The analogy might go even further in that there are judgements that both Emily and Felix can make concerning what is known as the 'spacetime interval' between the two events, something which, unlike simultaneity, is the same for both of them and indeed for all such observers. It might well be that, in the moral case, there are more general moral principles which aren't relative but which explain why it is that killing is wrong in one situation but not in another – perhaps a principle which says we should only kill in order to survive, or something along those lines, but something which applies to everyone absolutely. But we need not take this discussion any further. My point is that the notion of relativism *per se* does not imply that objective moral judgements cannot be made. Of course, it is still *compatible* with the view that anything goes, and if you already think that morality is like that, then you still can. But it is not the notion of relativism *as such* which forces such a stance.

way leads to us forgetting ourselves and making all sorts of unacceptable concessions. Rather, we should ask, 'What should I, as a rational person who has tried to be as informed as possible, do in this situation?' It is hard to imagine any situation in which it would be morally permissible, under these circumstances, to discriminate against or persecute individuals solely on the basis of their colour, sex or sexuality, since the myths on which such prejudices are based is not worthy of belief, and rational people should say so whenever a good opportunity arises. However, we may well be prepared to acknowledge that infanticide, involuntary euthanasia and enforced abortion would be legitimate ways for a society to survive times of hardship and over-population, or that marriage at thirteen would be legitimate at a time when life expectancy was around thirty years. However unpalatable these things would be in our present situation, it is not hard to make a case for them when the situation changes (so long as there were good reasons and they were not just done as an unnecessarily cruel punishment or because of a widespread belief that the person had been possessed by demons, was disapproved of by God or some such rubbish).

To get back to our topic of how we should treat animals, no matter what other people in other situations do to them, we should ask ourselves whether *our* treatment of them given *our* circumstances is legitimate. We certainly cannot expect to conclude anything meaningful about that from how the lion treats the zebra!

So these popular arguments, based around considering the moral deliberation – or rather *lack* of moral deliberation – of animals, do not work. Nevertheless, there is a popular theory of justice that requires that individuals deliberate on what would be agreed upon by rational individuals under certain conditions. By extension, some have thought that many, if not all, of our moral notions (not only justice) can be grounded in this way. According to this view, anything that is to be accorded moral consideration requires the capacity to deliberate; that is, it requires the capacity to enter into contracts with others. This popular theory deserves its own section.

SWINE ON THE DOTTED LINE: CONTRACTS WITH ANIMALS

The view that morality is in some way based on agreements between individuals does not rely on the idea of there being a time when such an agreement was explicitly made. It is more of a theoretical framework that helps us see what grounds our moral claims. The most influential formulation of this idea (as applied to the concept of justice) is given by the American political philosopher, John Rawls (1921–2002). In his *A Theory of Justice* (1971), he imagines that all parties to the agreement are placed behind a 'veil of ignorance', meaning that nobody knows their particular social status, talents, sex, sexuality, what property they have or at what period of history they live. Since each person does not know what situation they will find themselves in, they choose the rules according to what would be in their self-interest if they were in *any* of those situations (such as if they found themselves as an unemployed man, or woman seeking promotion in a male-dominated environment). Rawls argues that the rules to govern individuals that would be agreed upon under these circumstances would be fair, since they are those that would be agreed upon by rational individuals who start from a position of impartiality.

Where do animals fit into this picture? In this view, because only rational individuals are involved in determining the moral rules, based on their self-interest under the various scenarios in which they may find themselves, only rational individuals will be given any rights. We cannot ask 'What if we were animals?', because that would require us to deliberate about what we would rationally do if we were non-rational, which is of dubious sense. So, since for the sake of the argument we are assuming animals to be non-rational, this leaves animals with no rights. The obvious question is: why wouldn't the rational individuals choose rules on behalf of the animals? Peter Carruthers, who tries to extend Rawls' contractualist theory of justice to morality in general, argues that first, this would then give animals and humans *equal* rights (because there would be no way of giving them consideration without giving them equal consideration, since no prior moral beliefs about the lesser moral standing of animals are allowed behind the veil of ignorance), and that second, there is then nothing stopping these individuals choosing on behalf of other non-rational things, such as plants or rocks, and giving them equal rights (see Carruthers 1992: 99). Both these consequences are, for Carruthers, 'extreme' and 'acceptable to no one'. But if they are, we need to find reasons for thinking them unacceptable *within* the current contractualist framework, otherwise it does not capture everything there is to capture concerning moral evaluations; something else must be being appealed to. It is hard to see, within the framework, what could rule out extending rights in this way. Carruthers notes that no prior moral beliefs about the moral standing of animals (and the rest) are allowed behind the veil of ignorance, thinking this supports his view. But it seems to me that one can argue the other way: that far from supporting his view, this completely undermines it – *why* should such an extension of rights to animals (and the rest) be 'acceptable to no one' if we are choosing behind a veil of ignorance and not helping ourselves to any moral beliefs? If we do want to say that such an extension is unacceptable, it rather shows that the framework we are employing is not up to the job, since it does not by itself rule out such an extension.

Suppose we say, for the sake of the argument, that morality is best conceived as involving relations only between *rational* individuals. Carruthers endorses this concept, because it maintains 'a coherent vision of the nature and source of morality' without which it would 'no longer [be] clear what morality *is*' (Carruthers 1993: 100). However, the fatal flaw with this way of excluding animals is that it throws out the baby with the bathwater – literally – for this view will have trouble telling a plausible story about how young children fit into this framework for morality. And not only young children; it has trouble accommodating the senile, the mentally impaired, people in a coma and any other person who does not count as rational in the way that a normal adult human is.

At this stage, contractualists resort to desperate strategies to incorporate these categories. For instance, they may say that children *will* turn into rational agents, and rational adults can certainly be harmed by what happened in childhood.[16] But

[16] Following the argument of the death chapter, if the future branches, then it cannot be true at any time that a particular person will be harmed by a given act. In this case, we must understand the harm as meaning a past event caused harm to the particular rational individual. This is compatible with what has been said about harms so far. Things get complicated, however, when we consider future generations, as we shall see in the next chapter.

what about mentally impaired children? Or normal children who grow up to be mentally impaired adults? Or children who die young from disease? None of them are protected by rights within this framework. What exactly is wrong with using a non-rational human for experimentation and then killing him or her for food before they become rational? No rational person has been harmed, since there is no future rational person who was previously that child. If it is rationality that matters, there is no basis for thinking that any harm has been done. The same applies to the mentally impaired. Does this accord with our intuitions? If not, then this casts doubt on the contractualist framework for morality. And what about the senile? We cannot argue that they can be brought into the fold because they will become rational people; they won't. The only real way for contractualists to deal with this is to say that senile people still have interests.[17] However, since they are not rational, it follows that interests do not require rationality, in which case, animals cannot be ruled out as having moral status either. Contractualists cannot have it both ways.

The whole contractualist approach to these points is completely baffling. Why contractualists think they have to bend over backwards to accommodate the senile, the young, and so on, is a mystery. Not that it is baffling to want to include the senile and the young, but baffling why, *from the point of view of a contractualist*, they would want to include them. The long and the short of it is that if rationality is the important factor, then feeling the need to accommodate the non-rational, whether human or not, makes no sense. The basis for the moral

[17] I say more about interests in the next chapter.

intuition to include children and the senile cannot be anything to do with rationality.

Contractualists might argue that we should include all humans, whether rational or not, because to include all humans reinforces our positive disposition to treat all rational humans well. In other words, if we do not include children, the mentally impaired and the senile, then, humans being humans, we may well withhold rights from 'those who are sexually or intellectually "deviant" or from those whose intelligence is low' (Carruthers 1992: 116). This is a woefully poor argument. There is no conceptual reason why people who do not extend rights to non-rational things (and understand why) would go on to discriminate against rational things. Perhaps, as a matter of fact, humans would discriminate despite there being no conceptual link: this is doubtful. A person who would be so unreflective as not to understand the basis for the distinction between adults and young children would presumably be the sort of person who is taught the *results* of the moral framework rather than the reasons for it (much like children are taught that it is wrong to do such-and-such without being given a reason). The obvious way to teach that sort of person is to show them examples of normal adults and examples of children and say that things of the first kind have rights but things of the second kind do not. Why would we think that they would, under this kind of tuition, be stupid enough to confuse a baby with a normal gay adult or a senile person with a normal Jewish woman and argue that 'babies do not have rights, therefore there can be no moral objection to the extermination of Jews, Gypsies, gays and other so-called "deviants" ' (Carruthers 1992: 115)?

If we are speculating about the consequences that, as a matter of fact, might follow from excluding some individuals from moral consideration, there is just as strong an argument for extending rights to animals, for those who, as a matter of fact, are cruel to animals might also be cruel to humans. Should we give animals equal rights because if we don't, those who go hunting or bear-baiting might direct their viciousness towards innocent humans? I see no reason why they would turn on humans any more than I can see why excluding young children from the moral system would lead to discrimination against gypsies. Contractualists cannot have it both ways: either they include non-rational creatures like young children, and so animals as well, or they exclude them both. They can't use the weak indirect argument – that children should have rights because otherwise it might undermine the rights of other humans – to include young children, since such a fudge can be just as easily be used in favour of extending rights to animals.

Nevertheless, suppose we adopt Carruthers' suggestion that, although animals do not have any moral standing, they nevertheless have value. Carruthers writes:

> Ancient buildings, oak trees and works of art matter greatly to many of us without ... having moral standing. It is hardly sensible to say that a medieval castle, the oak on the village green or the *Mona Lisa* have a moral right to be preserved. Nor is it plausible to claim that we have moral duties with respect to these things ... Things that lack moral standing may nevertheless have indirect moral significance, giving rise to moral duties in a round-about way ... Even the legitimate owner of a medieval

castle may be under a moral obligation not to destroy it, since this would deprive present and future generations of a source of wonder and of attachment to the past. So even if we were to agree that animals lack moral standing, it would not follow that we can, with impunity, treat animals as we please. For there may still be indirect duties towards animals arising out of the legitimate concerns of animal lovers.

Carruthers (1992: 1–3)

The first thing to note is that it is not at all obvious that it is implausible to include 'ancient buildings, oak trees and works of art' in the moral sphere (this will be discussed in the next chapter) but, if they are excluded, it is not at all clear that the nature of animals is such that they fall on the side of ancient buildings, oak trees or works of art rather than on the side of humans. As Robert Nozick (Nozick 1974: 35) asks, 'Have animals the moral status of mere *objects*?' Do we really think that the only constraints on what we may do to animals concern the effects our actions have on 'animal lovers' or on present and future generations (which are the only constraints Carruthers mentions)? This cannot be right, since if we valued animals for the sense of wonder they induce in present and future generations, so long as some were protected, the rest could be used as humans wished. And what about ugly, unremarkable cows? What is there to protect them?

Neither does it help to invoke the feelings of animal lovers. What is wrong with owning your own cow, taking it to a very private area where nobody will find you and kicking it in the udders, nailing its tongue to a board and then cracking it over the head so that it bites its tongue off and breaks its teeth? If animal lovers know nothing about this, there is absolutely nothing wrong with it. It is an understatement to say that this strikes me as the wrong answer. Another option is to argue that it harms the interests of animal lovers, even though they never hear of it (in the sense we discussed in the chapter on death) but then we'd be in the position of having to weigh up the interests of animal lovers against the interests of someone who wishes to do whatever they like with their own property. If animals are not given moral standing in their own right, it is hard to see why the interests of animal lovers can come close to competing with the interests of the owner.

Carruthers makes much of what is known as 'reflective equilibrium' (an idea first expounded by Rawls). When we construct an ethical theory, we should start with common-sense moral beliefs and try to capture them within a theoretical framework, after which we see what the theoretical framework entails. If it entails something that seems unacceptable, we go back to the drawing board. The idea is to get some balance (hence 'equilibrium') between our common-sense beliefs and our theoretical framework. When we have constructed a framework that captures most of our intuitions in this way, we should follow what it prescribes. It seems to me that any ethical theory that does not say kicking a cow in the stomach, nailing its tongue to a board, and so on, is wrong is not yet at equilibrium. Unlike the cow, the right ethical theory hasn't yet been hit upon.

The most sensible conclusion we should draw is not so much that contractualism is wrong but rather that it cannot be generally applied to all morality. Rawls only went so far as to try to give an account of justice, and we may well think that this is correct: we might be able to accept that our treatment of young children, the senile and animals is not a question of just and unjust treatment. Nevertheless, we may still hold that they can be subject to moral and immoral treatment. In other words, we should conclude that the contractualist framework may well exhaust our concept of justice (this is an open question) but it certainly does not exhaust all there is to morality.

TAKING STOCK

Where does this leave us? There is good reason for ascribing a certain mental life to animals: they can be said to have beliefs and desires and to feel sensations such as pain. We left it open whether they could truly be said to deliberate on their actions but showed that even if we assume that animals are not rational in this way, this should not rule them out of having moral standing.

However, we need to ask about the *extent* of their moral standing. For utilitarians, what matters for having interests is the capacity for feeling pain and pleasure. Does that mean that humans have no more standing than animals? Not quite. Although, for Bentham, the sole factor in determining moral standing is the capacity for pain and pleasure, later utilitarians, such as John Stuart Mill (whose 'Harm Principle' we met in the last chapter) distinguish 'higher' from 'lower' pleasures. Mill writes:

> Few human creatures would consent to be changed into any of the lower animals, for a promise of the fullest allowance of a beast's pleasures; no intelligent human

being would consent to be a fool, no instructed person would be an ignoramus, no person of feeling and conscience would be selfish and base, even though they should be persuaded that the fool, the dunce or the rascal is better satisfied with his lot than they are with theirs.

(Mill 1861: 211)

Although many will empathise with these sentiments, they lead to some consequences with which we may not be so happy. What should I do if I find myself in a sinking boat and can only save one other living thing: a dog, a close but unintelligent friend or a cultured and intellectually gifted person? It would seem that Mill's statement gives a clear answer to the question: save the cultured person, so long as the quantity of the pleasures each of them has the capacity to experience are roughly the same (whatever that means). Is there an argument for saving the dog? There is if you think dogs can be close friends but let's set this aside and consider something Mill says later: '... a being of higher faculties requires more to make him happy, is capable probably of more acute suffering and is certainly accessible to it at more points, than one of an inferior type' (Mill 1861:212). So, although the cultured person may have better-quality pleasures, they also have more acute pains; it is difficult to see how a clear calculation of whose life is better in terms of pleasures and pains can be made. Neither does choosing the cultured person instead of the friend seem the right answer to me. I say 'save the friend' but this is based on framing morality more in terms of loyalty and solidarity than any utilitarian calculation. This intuition can also be captured by utilitarian thinking. Indeed, Mill thought that cultivating friendships and other special relationships with people would lead to greater overall happiness. So, utilitarianism could be used in support of incompatible answers on this issue and does not give clear recommendations in this case.

The case of the sinking boat may be rather far-fetched. Let us illustrate the difficulties we get into when formulating a consistent ethical position by considering a more down-to-earth case. Riding along a deserted road in the middle of nowhere, you come upon a stranded motorcyclist with a badly wounded leg. Unless the motorcyclist reaches a hospital right away, amputation may be unavoidable. You've made important plans of your own, and to take the motorcyclist to hospital would cost you time, bother and quite a bit of money. Nevertheless, it is likely that you would do what most of us would do and take them to hospital. Suppose that the next day, you receive a letter from UNICEF, asking for a donation of a few pounds to help save the lives of children living in a remote and poverty-stricken place. It takes just a couple of minutes to send a bit of money; far less time, bother and money than it cost you to save the wounded motorcyclist's leg and you know that your contribution would make a difference. Nevertheless, it is likely that you would do what most of us do: shove the letter in the bin.

Does this show that we are inconsistent and that morality demands that we should send the money to the children? If so, why stop there? Shouldn't we send all the cash we do not need for essentials to save those children? This is what we should be doing according to the philosopher Peter Unger (1995). However, Lewis (1996) thinks that these cases do not show that we are inconsistent but rather that they show us something interesting about the nature of morality, namely that it is a rather local affair. He takes the fact that utilitarians get into the position of thinking that we have to give away our spare cash (and indeed beg, borrow and steal to save the children) to be a reason for thinking that morality cannot be like this. We have no reason to think that helping the motorcyclist in front of us with the wounded leg is right, while not helping starving children miles away is not. The danger in this position is in trying to draw the line concerning just how local is local; plenty of people do not extend their morality much outside their own homes.

We are caught between two extremes but it is hard to find where in the middle we should come to rest. It seems to me that the best we can do (since even a rather large book probably wouldn't settle this issue) is to plump for a pragmatic position. It is difficult to see that any acceptable moral principles can be formulated to cover all problematic cases. Nevertheless, there are certain things we value that must be taken into consideration when we are deciding what we should do. What morality requires is for us to be sensitive to these features and do our best. We are complex creatures and there is no reason to think that we don't – and every reason to think that we do – have conflicting values. We have to balance them. Extreme views, either ultra-utilitarian or ultra-egoistic can be dismissed not because they are inconsistent – they have, after all, much more of a chance to be consistent than any view that lies in the middle ground! – but because they are insensitive to the weight of the various considerations involved. We are perhaps better off dropping the popular view of morality as a system of rules and adopting a view of morality as involving an ability to make the right decision for a particular occasion, based on particular features of the situation to which we are sensitive. And we should cultivate our characters, so that we approach all our decisions with integrity and honesty.

How does this pan out in how we treat animals? I think different things should be said about different areas: the considerations of using animals in important medical research are different from using them in cosmetic testing. To give a critical assessment of all the different ways in which animals are used would take a while and is not what we, as motorcyclists, are particularly interested in. So let me just say a few things that should be taken into consideration about those areas relating to leather.

Someone once said that people are more violently opposed to fur than leather because it's safer to harass rich women than motorcycle gangs. Of course, this joke isn't even remotely true (or funny) but there is something in its fundamental message that there is no difference between wearing fur and wearing leather. Fur is obtained through either hunting or farming. Hunting is done either for the fur itself or as a means of pest control while farming is done solely for the fur, since we generally do not eat the animals whose fur is used. Leather is mostly a by-product of the food industry, from animals that have either been farmed or hunted. (Hunting is sometimes called 'sport' yet doesn't fit the criteria for sport: there are no rules and one side doesn't know that it's playing. As P. G. Wodehouse wrote: 'The fascination of shooting as a sport depends almost wholly on whether you are at the right or wrong end of a gun.') When it has been obtained from hunting, leather is no different from fur.

There are certain aspects of hunting that many value; we do not, for instance, want to be over-run by vermin. Nevertheless, some ways of going about things are better than others. It is grossly disingenuous of those who ride around on horses and surrounded by a pack of hounds to claim that it is solely an exercise in pest control. This aspect of hunting is, at most, secondary; the primary aim being entertainment. I doubt that any honest person can make a case for this being justified. Hunting also occurs when not done in the name of pest control, such as in the case of certain bears. It is hard to believe that people will pay to have endangered species killed purely so they can grind up their penises for some ridiculous 'medicine' and then wear their fur. Again, this has no real justification.

What about farmed animals? Let us first dismiss the usual argument, sometimes put forward to justify using farmed animals, that that is what they have been bred for and they wouldn't have existed otherwise. We wouldn't use the same reasoning for humans. Is it acceptable to use certain people as slaves because we grew them for the purpose, even if they hadn't existed otherwise? (This is not to say that I wouldn't welcome the day when humans without brains could be bred specifically for use in those experiments for which animals are currently used. So long as the brain wasn't relevant to the experiment, this would by-pass our usual concerns over using animals, both in terms of sound scientific methodology and ethics. Such creatures would not have as significant interests as any animal, yet would be the closest thing to humans on which to conduct experiments.)

If we accept that animals do feel and have desires, then we must say that they should not be subject to pain and suffering, since this is a harm. So, farmed animals should not be subject to this kind of suffering, for whatever purpose. It is not good enough to appeal to the trivial pleasures got from it. Consider this case:

[A] Dalmatian dog is dragged out of a cage and into the alley behind Chilsung market in Taegu, South Korea. As a rope tightens around its neck, the dog defecates from shock. A metal rod connected to an electric generator is shoved into its mouth and electricity surges through its frame. The process is repeated several times. Stunned but not dead, its entire body is seared with a blowtorch to burn off the fur. The whole procedure lasts an hour. Its purpose is to make the dog secrete as much adrenaline as possible at the moment of death. The adrenaline-rich meat is believed to be a powerful aphrodisiac, giving men long-lasting erections ... While the meat spoils quickly if not refrigerated, the erection, legend has it, can last for hours.

(Taken from Mustienes and Hilland (eds.) 2006: 44)

I need not comment on this. Yet, if animals live a relatively pain-less life and if pain is the only harm they are capable of, it is per-missible to kill them for food, or for leather, or fur, so long as it is a painless death and we can establish that death is not a harm for them. Death is not a harm for them, unless they can have the same sort of interests that we said were subject to being frustrated in our earlier discussion of death. Can they desire that their lives, or those of their offspring, go a certain way or even that they desire to continue having the life that they currently enjoy? It isn't clear that, given their limited capacity, animals can reflect on those desires. Even if some apes can be said to be rational, this says noth-ing about those animals that are more usually eaten and used for leather. However, it isn't clear that they *can't* be rational, espe-cially mammals. We just don't know. Just because they can't reflect on their desires doesn't mean they do not have them. What matters are interests, not desires (I may desire something not in my interest or have an interest in something I do not desire) and it makes sense, to me, to say that the cow has an interest in carrying on living and death takes this away. Even if we are only concerned with not killing those creatures who have reflective capabilities, given that there is much at stake, we should be cautious in our treatment of animals. We certainly shouldn't kill animals for trivial ends. I, for one, endorse vegetarianism as the position to adopt. It's easy nowadays to be a vegetarian, it's healthy and it goes some way to reducing needless suffering. But it may well be that eating meat from ethically run farms does just as much in this regard; it depends on what we say about the harm of death.

What about leather? There are similarities between food and leather: both can look and smell fantastic. But it seems to me that there are also relevant differences between eating meat and wearing leather. Leather is an ideal material for motorcyclists: it is safe and it can last for many years. Contrast this with food, which requires a continual supply of animals. The difference between eating meat and wearing leather is, then, one of degree; each person must make up their mind where, along this scale, it becomes permissible to use animals, given the other things they value. A strict vegan who buys substantial amounts of leather each week is perhaps doing no better than a meat-eater who only wears clothes made from hemp. Perhaps a very occasional meat dish and a very occasional leather riding jacket and matching gloves fit best with the majority of the values we hold. Perhaps the person who does the best job of reconciling our desires is one who, eating meat or wearing leather, only uses that from wild animals who are killed painlessly because they are vermin (such as kangaroos, whose leather is now being widely used in motorcycle clothing). It seems a waste not to use the meat or skin if the animals are killed for pest control. I am not suggesting a revisionary approach to what we value but simply suggesting that people reflect more on the values that they already have. We want to live life to the full but none of us want to be the cause of unnecessary suffering. These values conflict. But we do not need to adopt an ascetic life to reduce significantly the amount of suffering that we cause. That solution would be as dreadful as leading a life of over-indulgence. I suggest that we find a healthy balance between virtue and vice. At the moment, the balance is tipped too far over to the wrong side. Hopefully, people will have seen that, when they reflect on what they care about, animals fit those criteria and that our present treatment of them conflicts with such core values. I would certainly welcome a shift to this more moderate and pragmatic approach to the treatment of animals. It would be a vast improvement on the situation we have at the moment.

It just remains to counter another popular objection to worrying about the moral status of animals. Carruthers writes:

> ... the cost of increasing concern with animal welfare is to distract attention from the needs of those who certainly do have moral standing – namely, human beings. We live on a planet where millions of our fellow humans starve or are near starving and where many millions more are undernourished. In addition, the twin perils of pollution and exhaustion of natural resources threaten the futures of ourselves and our descendants. It is here that moral attention should be focussed. Concern with animal welfare, while expressive of states of character that are

admirable, is an irrelevance to be opposed rather than encouraged. Our response to animal lovers should not be 'If it upsets you, don't think about it' but rather 'If it upsets you, think about something more important'.

(Carruthers 1992: 168)

This argument is ill thought-through. We can see this from considering the environmental impact of rearing animals.[18] One argument against using animals for food is that the amount of food obtained from an animal is very low, compared with the amount of food it consumes. This shouldn't matter, since cows eat grass and humans can't use grass as a source of food. This process looks to be a rather efficient way in which humans can convert non-food into food. However, things are not that simple. Animals in confinement have to be fed; they do not graze. Food – much more food than they themselves provide – has to be grown for them; food, such as corn, which humans could eat directly. So this is, in fact, a highly *in*efficient and wasteful way to generate food. But the inefficiency and waste will carry very little weight for a meat eater who judges the delicious end product to be worth it; and it is not as if, in developed countries, there is such a shortage of food that waste matters. Meat eaters may argue that we certainly can afford the luxury of squandering some food for the sake of having meat, but the idea that food could be used so inefficiently, when there are so many starving people in the world who could be fed by it, strikes many as too selfish for words. Yet there are still those who do not feel it is an obligation of their country to feed the starving people of others. Even without the extra food which could be used to feed humans

---

[18] See Singer (1975: chapter 4).

instead of animals, there is arguably enough food in existence to feed the starving, and yet they still starve.

The issue of how to tackle starvation will take us too far away from our main concern; suffice it to say that Carruthers' position is naïve. Furthermore, his comments (of particular interest to motorcyclists) on pollution and depletion of natural resources are inadequate, since these are also related to the rearing of animals and show that a concern for the well-being of humans requires a drastic reduction in animal use by humans. Not only is the rearing of food-animals an inefficient waste of primary food, it is a waste of energy in the conversion of that food (e.g. corn) into food (meat) and a waste of water and finite resources, such as fossil fuels, to manage the animals and produce the crops that feed them. Just tending to crops for human consumption would drastically reduce the demand on resources.

Animals also produce a lot of pollution themselves but the most worrying environmental impact of animal rearing is the vast amount of forests that have been felled to create land for animals and their food. Trees keep in check the amount of carbon dioxide in the atmosphere: fewer trees means more carbon dioxide in the atmosphere and more carbon dioxide leads to global warming. The felling of trees and the burning of fuels means that the animal industry is contributing to environmental disaster. Our use of animals, far from being irrelevant to the things that Carruthers mentions we should all be worried about, is central to a proper solution to the problems. Everyone, then, should be concerned with our use of animals, even those who have no concern for anything but human well-being. We shall discuss the relationship between motorcyclists and the environment in the next chapter.

Image 5. 'Look at you, bike!' Colin's Honda 50 gets a make-over of autumn leaves in *Heartlands* (2002)

Fifth Gear

160
180
200

Can tree huggers have rear huggers? Our obligations to the environment and future generations

> In the end, our society will be defined not only by what we create but by what we refuse to destroy.
>
> John C. Sawhill

Most motorcyclists require roads and those who don't will either be tearing up the countryside on dirt bikes or racing round on a purpose-built track that may well have been a vast area of green and pleasant land. Not only that, we all burn fossil fuels, contributing to global warming and, to top it off, we make quite a lot of noise in the process. These are things traditionally frowned on by environmentalists. Is it possible to reconcile the value of protecting the environment with the value of protecting our liberty, as motorcyclists, to do as we wish?

One way in which it might be argued that human freedom can legitimately be restricted would be to argue that the action in question has harmful effects on other humans. According to this view, the environment is valuable only in so far as it serves the needs of humans; to pollute the air with fumes and noise must be restricted not because it is a bad thing in itself to harm the *environment* but simply because it harms other *humans*. This argument for restricting the liberty of humans has a similar basis to arguments we have already tackled: if people are being kept awake at night because of revving engines and wheel spins, or are subject to high levels of harmful exhaust emissions, there is an argument for restricting the liberty of the motorcyclist to carry on. (It must be a reasonable requirement, of course. Someone who wishes to spend the afternoon in bed perhaps has weaker grounds for making demands on the motorcyclist.) So long as no other human is harmed by acting in this way, there is no argument for stopping this individual from continuing. This is all familiar territory from the chapter on speeding and helmets and need not be discussed in any more detail here.

However, many people do think that we can harm the environment independently of any harm that this does to any human. The first thing we need to do to settle the question of the legitimacy of restrictions on our riding activities is to establish what are the sort of things to which we can be said to have obligations. We saw in the last chapter that we should extend our ordinary moral practice and concern to incorporate non-human animals, since there was seen to be no morally relevant difference between them and us. Since non-human animals are certainly affected by environmental change, their interests must be taken into consideration here as well but as we have already discussed them, we need not do it again. Rather, our new interest comes from considering whether it makes any sense to do a similar thing and extend our moral concern to *other* non-human individuals; not just to non-human animals but to other living things, such as plants and fungi a nd perhaps even non-living things, such as mountains and rivers?[1]

NOT MUSHROOM FOR OBLIGATIONS, OR DO TREES HAVE STANDING?

In what sense can we extend moral consideration to individuals which are not animals? Although we use trees to make written contracts, a contract allegedly made *with* a tree wouldn't be worth the paper it was written on. However, this shouldn't stop us from thinking that the branch of moral consideration is thereby broken and cannot be extended to trees, since we saw in the last chapter that contractualism was a rather flawed way of grounding morality anyway. But neither can a framework based on experiences of pain and pleasure (such as certain forms of utilitarianism) be invoked: trees do not experience pain. Some might dispute this but our practice of ascribing painful states to various things does not easily accommodate objects

---

[1] One response that is sometimes put forward by feminists and mystics is to identify ourselves with nature, to be 'at one' with it. Somehow this is meant to stop us from destroying nature; but if we identify ourselves with it, then, as we can with our non-mystical selves, we can harm it like it's nobody's business. So even if we adopted the position, it wouldn't help the environmentalist cause.

such as trees. We saw in the last chapter that an alien with an entirely different nervous system to ours, who displayed an aversion to certain sorts of treatment in the way we would were we to consider ourselves in pain, could be considered to be in pain. It wouldn't be so much that trees do not have a physiological make-up like ours, if the tree displayed behaviour that we associated with being in pain, but without any such behaviour *and* no physiological grounds for thinking that it must be in pain even though it isn't displaying it in typical ways, the tree does not satisfy *any* of our criteria for being in pain and so can't be. It is as legitimate to call certain responses from the tree 'pain' when it is cut into with an axe as it is to say that a motorcycle feels pain (much like a Chinese burn?) when the tachometer registers the twist of the throttle.

Let us suppose that trees and their like cannot feel pain. Is there nevertheless a way in which they still qualify as falling within the scope of our moral concepts as we commonly employ them? As we saw in the last chapter, Peter Singer claims that animals should fall within the scope of our moral consideration because animals satisfy our idea of what it is to have interests. For Singer, the capacity to have *experiences* is a *necessary* condition for having interests and so it follows that trees, because they do not have experiences, cannot have interests. As we saw, what he needs for his argument to work in favour of animals being given moral consideration is for experiences to be *sufficient* for having interests, which says nothing about them being necessary. We might just add that experience must also be necessary for having interests but since this is precisely what is being questioned, it is no good to assert this without an argument. It seems perfectly natural to me to say that trees have interests: nobody would deny that they need water and sunlight, since without them they would die. Needs aren't always a matter of life and death but the notion of a need implies that without it, some goal is thwarted. For instance, we may need a good night's sleep to function properly in the morning but – however much it might feel like it at the time – we wouldn't die if we didn't. So, trees have needs and needs relate quite naturally to interests: having a need implies having an interest; in the case of the tree, an interest in having enough water and sunlight.

So, trees quite naturally qualify as having interests. And not only trees: all forms of non-animal life can be said to have interests, since they all need something to survive. The question is not whether they have interests but whether we should give them *equal* consideration of interest. Unless we are to be charged with speciesism, in the broader sense which now includes plant as well as animal life, we are compelled to do so: trees and their like have as much of an interest in having water as humans have. What impact should this have on our thinking – where do trees fit into the moral scheme of things? Should a human go without water for the sake of the garden? Should motorcyclists forsake roads in the interests of the countryside?

We need to establish what it is that environmentalists value before we can arbitrate between such competing interests. Although the common perception is that the environmentalist and the animal rights activist are one and the same – you'd expect a vegetarian to recycle bottles – the sorts of things valued by someone interested in protecting the environment and someone interested in animal welfare are often in tension. You'll hear environmentalists campaigning to save species and ecosystems and to preserve 'biodiversity' (the range of different kinds of plant and animal species). The tension between environmentalists' values and those of the animal rights movement emerges in cases where, to preserve certain species (the aim of environmentalism), individual animals, either from that species or another, may have to be sacrificed, perhaps by culling in times of over-population, which is something a campaigner for the rights of each and every animal is traditionally against.

What is taken to be the right action will be driven by what is taken to be the appropriate unit for evaluation: for the animal rights brigade, the unit will be *individual* animals, whereas for environmentalists the unit will be at the level of a *population*. This is perhaps why environmental ethics is difficult to ground, because our everyday morality is primarily geared towards our relationship to other individuals rather than to entities that, although they may comprise individuals, are distinct from them. Some people may feel love for, pride in or duty towards their family, country, university or football team and not just to the individuals that make them up. But note how different are these entities from the individuals that comprise them. A nation or a species may be composed of conscious individuals but the nation or species is not itself conscious and does not feel pain or emotion. To reverse the illustration, even though we are conscious, it is not true that our left earlobe or right buttock is. Wholes often have very different properties from their parts. Nevertheless, it is quite natural to say that an action can be in the interest of a nation or a species (again, perhaps to the detriment of a few unfortunate individuals) and so, in this regard, should be afforded equal consideration. We can see that there is potential tension between individuals and populations. Is it possible to give equal consideration to all these interests when some of them compete?

One way to resolve some of the tension would be to argue that the unit at the level of the species is more important than the unit at the level of the individual; that the value of biodiversity is greater than the value of any individual. I suspect that many of us have some sympathy with this. We certainly seem to think this is the case in aesthetics: it is not uncommon to value a rare piece of art more highly than we would do, on its merits, were it a more common kind of piece. Similarly, suppose there were two creatures, A and B, from two different species; A is a member of a species that is flourishing but B is one of the few remaining members of an endangered species. Would it be legitimate to sacrifice A not for the sake of saving B but to save the species of which B is a member? It is one thing having this intuition and quite another to justify the basis for it. Perhaps all we can say is that this kind of reasoning figures heavily in our value-judgements. But we also have conflicting intuitions. Suppose that we need to get across a river because our friend has fallen and is losing a lot of blood, and the only way to cross is to cut down the sole tree of its kind living. According to the environmentalist, we should not cut down the tree, since there are no more of them and plenty of humans, yet, according to most people, we should cut down the tree and save the person, showing that individuals are sometimes more valued than populations.

VIVE LA DIFFÉRENCE?

Those who argue for preserving biodiversity do so on a number of grounds. One, well-known, reason is the potential medicinal benefits. According to some estimates, although over a quarter of modern medicines are derived from tropical plants, only one per cent of tropical plants have been researched, leaving a huge potential for future pharmaceuticals. This is an argument that places the value of biodiversity in its potential benefit to humans. But if this is its sole value, it is legitimate to weigh it against other competing benefits to humans, such as roads and burning fuels. What makes it difficult to argue for preserving biodiversity on this basis is that we simply do not know what benefits these non-researched species would bring or how to weigh their uncertain benefits against the known (albeit moderate) benefits of building roads and using petrol. This argument from the potential medical benefits of biodiversity, then, does not *by itself* make the environmentalist position compelling.

Another argument for preserving biodiversity concerns the claim that, in an ecosystem, there is a delicate balance of symbiotic relationships between various species, such that were the balance upset, the whole system would crash. Recent scientific research disputes this: ecosystems seem to be far more robust than has been thought. This is a purely scientific question that must be left to scientists; the philosophical reservation is that this argument only works on the assumption that it would be a bad thing for the ecosystem itself to become extinct. This pushes the question back to what it is about the ecosystem that makes it valuable. Maybe it's that wiping out a whole ecosystem could lead to the climate of the earth changing, thereby endangering humans. If this is the real reason, we are again left with valuing biodiversity because, via a series of complex causal mechanisms, it may ultimately benefit human beings. But in so far as humans are not affected, according to this position, there would be nothing wrong in allowing species to become extinct. (And it may even be that, in so far as any humans are affected, it only affects future people; yet, as we shall see later, it is not clear whether allowing such a catastrophe to affect them can be considered wrong.)

The third way to argue for preserving biodiversity is different: biodiversity is taken to be valuable independent of any benefit it has for humans; it has *intrinsic* rather than *instrumental* value. Some people are rather sceptical of the notion of intrinsic value, thinking it sounds rather mystical. But all we need to say to characterise the notion is that something of intrinsic value is valued *for its own sake*; an end in itself. Contrast the value of money with the value of experiencing great music. Money is not valuable for its own sake but as a means or instrument to some end, whereas experiencing great music is just valuable in itself. (Great music may also have instrumental value, such as inspiring you to do something great but it needn't, to be valuable; if it does, this is a layer of added value, rather than its primary value.) The notion of intrinsic value, then, is far from mysterious.[2] Let's spend a little time getting straight about what it is and what it isn't.

[2] There is another sense of 'intrinsic' value that is sometimes used that means something like 'has value independently of its relation to anything else' and in this sense is opposed to 'extrinsic' value, rather than 'instrumental' value. I think that 'intrinsic' in the way I use the term captures a more significant notion and is probably what most people are getting at when they use the notion. For instance, many people may be inclined to think that a wilderness, untouched by human hands, has intrinsic value but since being untouched by human hands is a relational notion, they cannot be talking about the intrinsic versus extrinsic notion but must mean the intrinsic versus instrumental notion.

BILLY-NO-MATES, THE LAST HUMAN ALIVE

Consider a thought experiment. Suppose that, due to some pointless war between the Unbearably Arrogant Imperial Army and the Stupidly Intolerant People's Front, Billy is not only the last human left alive on the planet but also the last living animal – and knows that he is. He also knows that he will die in a few hours. He spends his remaining time lying quietly in the luscious green grass next to a gentle stream that originated from the nearby mountains, while contemplating what sheer destruction will result from his setting a timed device to detonate a series of nuclear bombs the next day at various locations across the world, such as in rain forests and mountain ranges. If you are sickened by the thought of what silly Billy is doing, you can't think that what he will destroy had only instrumental value: by the time it has been destroyed, it is of no use to any human.

Some try to draw a stronger conclusion from this thought experiment. Because we would think that the mountains and the rain forests would still have value even if humans became extinct, it shows that these things are valuable, independent of what any human thinks of them. However, this does not follow and it is, perhaps, this common running together of the notion of intrinsic value with values being *objective* or 'out there' in the world, existing independent of any human to value them that has led to people being suspicious of the notion of intrinsic value. It is a mistake to run the two things together; after all, we could each have a *subjective* idea of what things to value for their own sake, without thinking that it has any more basis than that, or we could take certain things to have intrinsic value because of some kind of *inter-subjective* agreement among a given community. Given this, we could interpret the 'last human alive' thought experiment thus: we think that Billy has done something dreadful, because the things he will destroy are things that we deem intrinsically valuable and we would judge them to be intrinsically valuable even if humans became extinct. This is different from saying that they would be intrinsically valuable independent of our judging them to be intrinsically valuable. If we are sceptical of the notion of objective value, we should not reject the notion of intrinsic value on the basis that it implies that values must be objective, since it doesn't. The notions of objective, subjective and inter-subjective value cut across the notions of intrinsic and instrumental value.

Now we have this in place, we can ask whether it is plausible to think of biodiversity as intrinsically valuable. In the subjective sense it is – there are plenty of people who think that biodiversity is to be valued for its own sake – but somebody's taking it to be intrinsically valuable is not a sufficient ground for preventing someone else acting against it. By contrast, if biodiversity is intrinsically valuable in an objective sense, then this *is* a sufficient reason for placing constraints on the actions of those who may spoil it.[3] Can a case be made for thinking that biodiversity is intrinsically valuable in the objective sense?

---

[3] Although, as Mackie (1977) notes, if such values are objective, we may not feel motivated to act on them. But this is what we require of value judgements in ethics; they have the feature of motivating us to either do something or refrain from doing it. How can something entirely external to you, motivate you to act in any way? Mackie says that to do this, objective values would have to be very 'queer', which is one reason why he does not believe they exist.

ARE TWO HEADS BETTER THAN ONE?

We have considered an extension of our moral consideration from individuals to groups of individuals. If bio-diversity is taken to be intrinsically valuable in an objective sense, it is hard to justify the distinction we draw between 'nice' species and 'nasty' ones. Many of us don't think twice about the bugs that spend their dying moments on our helmet visor or the bacteria killed during cleaning or by medicines (and wouldn't even if they were the last of their kind). Not many people lament the demise of the dinosaurs, but even if they do, does anyone think that lettuces have a shred of intrinsic value and would anyone shed a tear over an extinct ancestor of the onion?

We may be mistaken; we may be wrong not to value the diversity that such species bring, but it is hard to see why diversity, in itself, is more valuable. Why should we think, just because of the diversity, that a world in which humans grow only one head is less valuable than a world in which one species of human grows one head and another species grows two? (It seems to me that this would be a world where the instrumental value of having two heads could render it a much worse world despite the intrinsic value of the diversity. Think of the trouble you'd have sticking two helmets on.)

The case of the two species of human illustrates a subtle problem. Dividing individuals into species is, to a large extent, a *conventional* matter based on the interests of those doing the classifying. For instance, the question probably crossed your mind – but presumably just the one mind – of whether we should say we have two species of human, rather than one species of human that occasionally produces individuals with two heads. It seems to me that there is no fact to determine this issue; we just have to *choose* what to say on the basis of what it is most useful or interesting for us to say. In that case, the diversity of species must depend on the interests of the classifier, because how much diversity there is depends on how narrowly or broadly species are defined. This undermines the notion that diversity is objectively valuable, since diversity is ultimately fixed by convention and nothing that is an objective feature of the world is fixed by convention.

The inter-subjective account of the intrinsic value of biodiversity looks much more promising, since it seems to fit better with the idea that species are to some extent chosen (on the basis of what we find important) rather than discovered. Also, if a significant number of us buy into a common system of values, this acts as a much more forceful reason to curb some of our actions than the purely subjective preference for what is intrinsically valuable. An inter-subjective account seems to be the best direction in which to take the view that biodiversity is intrinsically valuable. There certainly seems to be widespread agreement that certain living things matter – and matter for their own sake rather than their usefulness to humans. It seems to me that there is widespread agreement on this both at the individual level and at the higher level of the species or ecosystem. Yet, as we have seen, these two things sometimes pull in opposite directions and it is hard to find any good reason for thinking that one has more importance than the other when they conflict. What should we do? Maybe all we can do is accept that sometimes there will be irresolvable disputes. This should come as no surprise; there is often inter-subjective agreement concerning what is valuable but no agreement over how to resolve tensions. In other words, it is common for humans to want to have their cakes and eat them. How far should we go with the inter-subjective account? And what implications does it have for motorcyclists?

ROAD HOGS VERSUS BIO-CHAUVINIST PIGS

If we go with the inter-subjective view, it does not look to be totally out of the question to assign intrinsic value to having a diversity of objects that aren't even living and even to assign intrinsic value to the individual objects themselves. Isn't it fair to say that there are plenty of people in agreement over the intrinsic value of an environment that includes mountains, rivers, deserts, canyons, waterfalls, marshland, stars, stalactites and other rock formations, glaciers (and maybe even icebergs and clouds)? This intrinsic value should place constraints on what we do if our actions damage such objects. Indeed, there is an argument that each object could even be morally harmed by our actions, since there is a case for saying that such objects have interests: rivers need rain, and it is against the interests of a stalactite to be smashed by a hammer. Should we take these interests seriously? If we follow the precedent of the arguments presented above, it seems that, if they have interests, those interests should be considered equally. Not to do so would lead to a charge analogous to speciesism: only to consider the interests of biological entities like animals and trees and to ignore the interests of non-biological entities like mountains and rivers is *bio-chauvinism*. As the Australian environmentalist philosopher, Robert Elliot, says:

> Consider a stalactite, an organised collection of mineral compounds created by natural processes over time. It is

not completely implausible to suggest that the stalactite is a natural item with a good of its own defined in terms of its organisation ... And, it might be added, in the case of the stalactite we are not considering an inert item, rather we are considering an item in the process of developing according to its kind. It might be that biological organisation is initially more obvious and impressive but, so the suggestion might run, it is the basic fact of organisation that counts.

(Elliot 1995: 14)

If this charge can be made to stick, the environmentalist movement looks to be on solid ground in demanding that we curb activities that are against the interests of mountains, rivers and deserts. Should we stop building roads and the racetracks on which to ride our motorcycles; stop tearing up the countryside on dirt bikes; stop mining the land for materials to build motorcycles; stop burning the fuels that contribute to further damage of the planet, not only of its living parts but also of the islands that will disappear and the rivers that will dry up? Must we stop immediately and recycle our motorcycle?

Although I am all for concern for the environment, these arguments are far from strong enough, both philosophically and factually, to get motorcyclists to change their ways. One philosophical reason is that everything that has been said so far can be said about motorcycles and their preservation too! Motorcycles *need* a surface on which to run, as well as fuel and oil to function properly and there are plenty of things which are not in their interest, such as to be washed with warm water after a run on a salty road. They also have an 'organisation' that far surpasses that of any stalactite. In short, motorcycles have as many needs and interests as the next object. To discriminate against them looks to be another form of chauvinism.

An environmentalist who wants to hold on to the idea that non-living objects can have interests may still emphasise the following reason for distinguishing mountains from motorcycles: mountains, unlike motorcycles, are *natural* objects. It is the fact that the objects are natural and that the diversity generated by them is natural, that forms the basis for assigning to them intrinsic value. It cannot be denied that calling something 'natural' is often used to indicate a valuable attribute. For instance, those who market foods, medicines or shampoos, use claims like 'all-natural ingredients' as a strategy to persuade us that they are better than 'non-natural' competing products. However, to appeal to the notion of naturalness, at least in this context, is useless. Not only is the distinction between natural and non-natural dubious but in any sense in which we might draw a distinction, it fails to bear any substantial moral weight. In what sense can anything that exists be considered unnatural? All the elements of a motorcycle have been taken from this world and, with the help of human ingenuity, rather than other-worldly spirits, have been stuck together to create something incredible. Precisely which part of this process is unnatural? And in what sense is the diversity generated by these objects unnatural?

The obvious response is to say that 'natural' means something like 'independent of human intervention'. Rain forests, mountains ranges, deserts and stalactites can take millions of years to evolve and will continue to evolve in a certain way if humans do not interfere; motorcycles and roads, on the other hand, would not have occurred without humans. So, it is not so much the materials involved in the creation that make one intrinsically valuable and the other not, and neither is it any difference in the needs and interests of these objects; rather, the difference is taken to lie in how these objects have come about.

We do indeed attach significance and value to the historical facts surrounding a given object. Suppose you go to the shops and buy a Picasso. You take it home and admire the brushwork and invite your cack-handed painter friend Rolf round for tea. While you're in the kitchen, Rolf accidentally drops a tin of paint over the Picasso; happily, famed for his high-speed reproductions of great paintings, Rolf produces another painting with the same brushwork. When you get back from the kitchen, you notice the smell of paint and a rather shifty-looking Rolf but you don't notice the difference between Picasso's painting and Rolf's – visually, they're identical. Nevertheless, most of us would think that because of its history, the Picasso is much more valuable and that Rolf has done great harm.

Elliot argues similarly in a deservedly celebrated paper (see Elliot 1982). Suppose that there is a proposal to mine a forest for certain minerals. Large areas of the forest are to be cleared of vegetation. All parties agree that the forest has a value quite apart from its instrumental value, so it is agreed that it would be a bad thing, considered in itself, for the forest to be dramatically altered. Acknowledging this, the mining company promises to restore the forest to its original condition after the minerals have been extracted – at least, it will be a very good likeness, minus the minerals. Elliot argues that, nevertheless, if this project goes ahead, there would be less value in the world, for something has been lost that could never be restored by the mining company, namely the link with the past and the particular way in which the original forest arose naturally.

I think many of us will have some sympathy with this; but it isn't clear that even this improved environmentalist position is decisive against the motorcyclist. What is the difference between a human constructing a road or a motorcycle, and an ant constructing an ant hill? All sorts of organisms construct their environment (and so change it into something that it wouldn't have been had they not interfered with it) but nobody thinks that what they create is any less valuable because they have created it. The obvious difference between the creation of ant hills and ecosystems, on the one hand, and roads and motorcycles, on the other, is that the latter are created by *conscious* beings. But, as the philosopher of biology Elliott Sober notes, it would be odd to think that something is *less* valuable simply because it was brought about through conscious deliberation and planning (see Sober 1986). Indeed, we often think things are *more* valuable when they have been deliberately done, rather than by accident or habit.

These are all philosophical reasons why motorcycles escape certain kinds of environmentalist arguments, but they are equally effective in showing how vehicles in general are not subject to such arguments. However, in appealing to factual matters concerning the motorcycle's relationship to the environment, we see how much better they fare than cars and how they should be embraced by environmentalists rather than demonised with the rest. First, one (or two) riders on an average motorcycle do not consume anywhere near as much fuel as someone who uses a car. Second, due to their manoeuvrability in traffic and the space they take up in a queue, congestion on the road would be vastly reduced if more people got out of their cars and got on a motorcycle. Third, the space needed to park motorcycles is nothing like that needed for cars. Fourth, encouraging more people to own motorcycles and use them as their primary mode of transport will reduce needless short journeys that could be walked (since the pay-off for going on a short journey is not worth the hassle of dressing for a motor-cycle journey). In short, if everyone used motorcycles for much of what they use cars, there would be no need to worry so much about depleted resources and pollution, or build new roads to ease congestion. Motorcycles should be embraced as part of the solution to some environmental problems. As someone once said, 'Life is too short for traffic.'

SEEING THE WOOD FOR THE TREES

Let us step back and see what has been shown. I started by showing how there are plenty of non-animal objects, both living and non-living, such as trees and mountains, which can be said to have value independent of their *uses* to humans, but further, that this does not necessarily commit us to thinking that they have value independent of humans *judging* them to be of value. Some environmentalists have taken this to support their view that we should stop harming the environment in mining and burning fossil fuels and in destroying countryside by con-structing more roads. However, we saw that, far from helping this particular environmental cause, arguing that objects have some intrinsic value in virtue of being natural backfires; it is hard to see what it rules out as having interests. Motorcycles have as much of a claim to flourish as any other inanimate object, according to these criteria. Does this mean that we could, with a clear conscience, start building more roads and burning as much fuel as we like? This does not follow, for there is equally no reason for thinking that the instrumental value of roads is more valuable than the intrinsic value of fields. (Very few roads have intrinsic value, once we have stopped thinking that naturalness – which everything in this world has – is an intrinsic value. Motorcycles, it seems to me, have both intrinsic and instrumental value, as we shall see the next chapter.)

We have a situation much like the one we had at the end of the last chapter, where we ended up with competing values but no real, principled, way of organising them. The situation we have here is much broader, since not only are we trying to juggle the values we attach to humans and animals but we also need to juggle the values we attach to everything else. We attach value to a wide variety of *individual* objects and also to *populations*, so not only do these disparate individuals compete with each other, they also compete with populations. If this weren't difficult enough, there is a variety of *kinds* of value they could have – aesthetic, economic, scientific, medical, recreational, historical – some of which are best seen as intrinsic values (aesthetic), some instrumental (economic), some both (recreational – done for its own sake but perhaps conducive to health). How do we compare the aesthetic value of an important new piece of architecture with the instrumental value of a new piece of hospital equipment, when there is only so much money to go around? In Table 1, I have compiled the kinds of things we might value and the ways in which we might value them. Thinking how to fill in the columns for each example falling under each kind of thing, when the values that fill those columns are so varied, and where to draw the line in withholding certain values from a particular example within a kind (indicated by a question mark in the Table) should put into perspective how complex is our system of values and how implausible it is to think that we can hope to have an entirely consistent view of things, if we are to be faithful to the sorts of things we value.

Table 1: Illustration of our complex system of values

Kinds of things we might value	Example	Intrinsic	Instrumental
Human animal	Me and you		
Non-human animal	Cow, dugong, squid		
Living non-animal	Tree, potato (?), bacteria (?)		
Non-living natural	Rock, desert, cloud (?)		
Non-living non-natural	Motorcycle, kettle (?)		
Human species/community	Present population of the earth, future population of the earth		
Non-human animal species/community	Gorillas, bears		
Ecosystem/Biosphere	Brazilian rain forest		
Geosphere	The whole planet, the Solar System (?)		

As I suggested in the last chapter, in the light of this, perhaps we should try to find some middle ground between (what is perceived to be) virtue and vice. In these times of increasing awareness of global warming, the use of vehicles is rather frowned upon; it is a perceived vice, but we have seen no really compelling argument for thinking that the interests of motor-cycles are any less important than the interests of trees. Equally, we saw no compelling reason to think that it is permissible to burn as much fuel as we liked. So, we should find a way of bal-ancing these values as best we can. We should cut out needless short journeys, push for alternative fuels (burning fossil fuels, after all, is not what we want to do but an unfortunate side effect of it), check the air pressure in our tyres, change the air filter regularly and try to resist – although this might be too optimistic! – accelerating too much. This goes for life outside the helmet too. We all value using electrical items but nobody is worse off for turning off lights and not leaving their computer monitors on standby. So long as we do our bit concerning needless waste, we should do those things which make life worth living – noting that all should be done in moderation – for we have encountered no good reason from environmental-ism why we should stop riding entirely, especially since it is a relatively environment-friendly means of transport and a truly life-enhancing way to travel.

Nevertheless, some might complain that it is all very well for me to say this now, since I won't be around when the shit hits the fan. What about all those people in the future, who will suffer because we have decided merely to reduce our harmful emissions rather than to cut out riding entirely? This issue of harm goes beyond the discussion of the chapter on helmets and speeding, where we were only considering our obligations to our human contemporaries, and is thus an important issue that needs to be tackled in its own right.

Fifth Gear

RESPONSIBILITIES TO FUTURE GENERATIONS

One question that might occur when we talk about our obligations to future generations is, 'How can we have obligations to people who do not exist?' This presupposes the controversial view that future people do not exist until they become present. However, a number of philosophers, perhaps even the majority, think that the future is as real as the present. We saw how this position panned out in the chapter on death. According to this view as applied to the past, Elizabeth I is as much a flesh and blood creature as are we; it is just that she is located at a different time (in almost the same way that Australia is real for those in the UK, despite its having a different location in space). This allowed us to see quite clearly how the interests of dead people can be affected after they have died. If we apply the same treatment to the future, our great-great-great-grandchildren, if we *will* have them, *do* exist as flesh and blood creatures; it's just that they are located at a future time.

However, we need not buy into this view of the future to establish whether we have any obligations towards future people; all we need is the fact that there *will* be future people. Suppose we plant a bomb that will go off 200 years from now and suppose that it will kill over a hundred people. It would be a poor defence to argue that the people who will be killed do not exist at the time the bomb was planted; the bomb's exploding would cause their deaths, just as clearly as would a bomb planted and set to go off on the same day. The present existence of future generations is neither here nor there.[4]

---

[4] However, as in the chapter on death, if we have a branching future, this does create some difficulty, and the nature of the causal connection itself

Whether or not we think future people exist, what we can't do is identify any *particular* future people in the way that we can past people. The best we can do in the case of future people is to make *general* claims about them: *someone or other* will be killed by this bomb.[5] The question is whether it matters that we cannot identify particular people towards whom we are wondering whether we have obligations. It shouldn't matter. If we plant the bomb today to detonate today, we might not be able to identify the particular people who will be killed. The best we can do is to say that *someone or other* will be killed. Yet we still have an obligation not to kill those people, whoever they may be. Thus, not being able to identify particular individuals to whom we have obligations is also neither here nor there.

If these factors are not important in distinguishing future people from our contemporaries, should we give them moral consideration? The question is: on what basis, and to what extent, should moral consideration be given? In the last

between the present and the not-yet-existent would have to be made sense of. For more on such matters, see my (2006a) book.

[5] There is a very good reason for this. It is common to think that genuine reference to particular individuals requires some kind of direct or causal connection with them. It is possible to have this with past people, since we can use a name which denotes them so long as the present use of the name lies at the end of chain of uses of the name that stretches back, in an appropriate kind of way, to the individual. (For an account of how those who do not believe in the existence of past can do this, see my (2006a) book.) But if reference requires this kind of connection, then reference to future individuals will not be possible since this would require a link from the future individual to the present use of the name, which amounts to requiring the direction of causation to run from later to earlier, which it doesn't (again, see my (2006a)). Of course, we might dub future individuals with something that looks like a name – 'Egbert', 'Cyril' and 'Ethel', for instance – but it wouldn't be genuine reference in the sense that we'd have some particular people in mind when we did it.

chapter, we discussed contractualism as a theory of morality. Contractualism cannot ground any obligations to future people since they cannot reciprocate, but does this mean we should adopt contractualism and conclude therefore that we do not have any obligations towards future people? If contractualism were a compelling theory on other grounds, maybe we should, but as we have seen, it isn't. I think our intuition that there *is* something wrong with planting bombs to detonate in the future has more weight than the prescription of the contractualist theory. Thus, I think we should take this to be another reason for thinking that contractualism is a flawed theory of morality.

We also discussed utilitarianism, and this seems a much more supportive framework for our intuition that future people count for something. Indeed, they count equally. Utilitarianism seems to give a clear answer to whether we should use today's resources to make our lives better, even though it would result in a situation where future generations are worse off: any decision concerning the environment should take the interests of future generations equally into account. Suppose that we destroy certain areas of the natural environment to build more roads and burn more fossil fuels to get our motors running. This works out better for us than for future generations: we do not have to invest in alternative new technologies, we do not feel the adverse impact of our actions and although we do lose some of the natural environment, at least we have had the experience of such an environment before we destroyed it. Should future people feel rather hard-done-by by our selfish decisions? Do we have an obligation to them to ensure that their lives, which should be given equal consideration of interest, are not made worse by our actions?

Things are not so simple. There is a complicating factor, yet to be addressed, that is of fundamental significance to the issue of our obligations to future generations and whether they can be said to have any moral claims over us. For it is not as if we have the same influence over our contemporaries as we do over future people; the significant difference between present and future people is the fact that *we* determine, to a large extent, *which* people exist in the future.

As the British philosopher, Derek Parfit, argues, had our mother waited a month before conceiving us, the child which would have been born (from a different egg and sperm) would have grown into a different person. Had slightly different conditions held, we would not have existed.[6] If our very existence is sensitive to the time at which we are born, it is plausible to think that choices we make now, particularly important ones concerning our impact on the environment, will have a dramatic effect on the future. The details of the lives of future people will be affected by what we do, which will in turn affect the details of the lives of even later people, and so on, until we reach the point where we can say that had we acted differently, different people would have existed (see Parfit 1984).

This looks like it has dramatic consequences for the consideration we should show towards future people. It looks as

---

[6] Do not confuse this with the argument in the death chapter on essentialism concerning the origins of a person. There we saw that if the origin were the same, then we could be born at a different time. Here, the origin is different and that's why we end up with different people. Also, in that case, we kept much of the world fixed over a short period of time and just altered the time of the birth but in this case we are dealing with complex knock-on effects of decisions that affect a wide number of people and considering its impact over a significantly longer time period.

though, had we not acted in the way we did, those future people who appear to be hard-done-by by us should, in fact, be rather grateful! Had we not depleted resources, history would have taken a different course and they would not have existed. They can hardly complain, then, that we have harmed them in any way.

Does it follow that we can, with a clear conscience, continue to do as we please, since most future people cannot be said to be harmed by our actions? I do not think so, for two reasons. The first is that even though no person is harmed, we may still think that things other than humans have been harmed. It may be that we are harming the environment itself, as we discussed earlier. In any case, the second reason for thinking this does not give us licence to do as we please is that, even though we cannot say that there are some future people such that we should have brought about a better life for *them*, it does not follow that we should not have brought it about that *someone* has a better standard of living.[7] Thus, even though no future individual can be said to have been harmed by our actions, we are at fault for not securing the best future for humanity: *other* people should have been brought into existence.

There are a number of assumptions concerning the choice to conserve resources and the environment rather than adopt a policy of depletion. Depletion might be a better strategy overall. It might force us to create new technologies sooner rather than

---

[7] In the technical jargon, it is a question of the *scope* of the quantifier. We must distinguish:

(a) someone is such that: it ought to be that: *they* had a better life, from
(b) it ought to be that: *someone* is such that: they had a better life.

In the context of our discussion, (a) is false. But even so (b) is true; and this is what should guide our actions concerning the future.

later, giving rise to a higher standard of living sooner rather than later. It might well be that global warming brings unforeseen benefits; perhaps some magnificent, extreme, environments for future ecologists and explorers to get as excited about as our contemporaries get about our environment, and for future environmentalists to be as passionate about preserving for generations in their future. Future generations may no more mourn the loss of certain species than we mourn the loss of the dinosaurs. They may even be grateful for the extra roads. Maybe: but this is far too speculative to be of any guidance. The only way in which we can proceed is to stick with what we know. We know what sorts of things we value in the environment, ourselves and other animals. We can bring into existence people who will value the things that we do. That much, we know, is worth trying to promote and preserve. Far too much is at stake to leave it up to chance. Can we be sure that these alternative environments will not be so extreme that nothing can survive? Can we be sure that there will be as diverse or as rich a variety of species? Can we be sure that the loss, through rising sea levels, of the islands of the Maldives (which are no more than six feet above sea level) that scatter the deep blue Indian Ocean with vibrant turquoise foreshores and white sandy beaches, is a worthwhile sacrifice for what will replace it (which is likely to be just more blue water)? What benefit could there be from the rising temperature of the oceans that could justify the cost of the consequent destruction of rich coral reefs? We could go on, with countless examples. Where does this leave us as responsible motorcyclists? Should we sacrifice our dream machines for the sake of future generations of people?

Why should we sacrifice our own desires for the sake of remote strangers? Just as in the discussion, in the previous chapter, between Lewis and Unger over the decision not to send money to starving children in a remote country, why should we sacrifice anything for those substantially separated from us in time? The relevant difference comes in there being someone who is harmed in the case of the starving children, whereas in the case of the future, there is no person who is harmed (in the sense explained above). However, this difference would seem to give us *less* reason for doing anything for future people – if we are not even prepared to do it for people who can be harmed, what chance have future people?

But it is best not to see environmental issues as a conflict between our wants and those of other people: as sacrificing our well-being for the sake of those with whom we have no personal ties. Rather, we should view any sacrifices we make as sacrifices we make *for ourselves. We* value certain things and *we* want them to continue (and we want others to value them but whether or not they do is a different matter). So what we should do is decide what is of value and try to preserve it, not for the sake of future generations but for our own sakes. We are, then, back in the same old complex business of balancing our present set of values. We have found a framework in which to conduct the discussion about what we should do to safeguard our planet for future generations. But nothing has been said, so far, to make us think that, so long as we continue in moderation, we are not right to continue riding our motorcycles.

We have concentrated so far on the value of human and non-human animals, as well as of the environment. It is now time to discuss the value of motorcycles themselves, specifically, the nature of their aesthetic value.

Image 6. The Comanche Helicopter motorcycle made by Orange County Choppers

Sixth Gear

From spare part to high art: the aesthetics of motorcycles

Art, like morality, consists in drawing the line somewhere.

G. K. Chesterton

Sexy, beautiful, breathtaking, elegant, striking, magnificent, charismatic, iconic. Anyone who knows anything about bikes knows that some, if not all, of these terms truly apply to certain motorcycles. The Ducati 916, the stunning work of designer Massimo Tamburini, was unveiled in the early 90s, stirring emotions which cannot be explained simply by noting its subsequent domination (with the help of its equally desirable successors, the 996 and the 998) of the World Superbikes competition. After all, other marques, such as Honda, did well in this competition and yet don't adorn as many bedroom walls (of middle-aged boys as well as the teenage variety) as the Ducati superbike. Even before it got on the track, the 916 was (and still is) seen as something special: even those ignorant of its rôle – never mind its importance! – on the track are rarely insensitive to the delicious sight of the twin mufflers of the upswept exhaust system tucked under the rider's seat, the irresistible, somewhat sinister, set of headlights set into the droop-snoot nose of the front fairing, the mouth-watering styling of the tank and the ultra-clean look of the tubular trellis chassis and single-sided swinging arm. I could go on.

Of course, the Ducati marque does not have a monopoly on style: the heart-stopping back end of the MV Agusta F4 (also designed by the genius, Tamburini), let alone the rest of the bike, is enough for even the coldest of fish to contemplate selling their children to put down a deposit on one. And so it goes for many great motorcycles. Beyond doubt, certain motorcycles are highly desirable objects, albeit to a relatively small – that is, discerning! – group of people. The question I wish to discuss is whether, to what extent and, most interestingly, *how* certain bikes function as genuine *works of art*, where I use 'work of art' positively to endorse an object as worthy of aesthetic appreciation. (I confess to a particular fetish for Italian marques and clearly think that my case applies to many of these motorcycles. Those with an interest – healthy or otherwise – for a different style, be it an American cruiser, a Japanese high performance 'crotch rocket' or a classic British invention, will be able to use my considerations to make the case for their own objects of affection.)

I suspect that I'm preaching to the converted but the controversy that surrounded the exhibition *The Art of the Motorcycle* (see T. Krens, *et al.* 2001) at the Solomon R. Guggenheim Museum, New York (26 June–20 September,

1998), the Field Museum of Natural History, Chicago (7 November, 1998–21 March, 1999), the Guggenheim Museum Bilbao (24 November, 1999–3 September, 2000) and the Guggenheim Las Vegas (Autumn 2001), is enough to show that it is not readily accepted that bikes are legitimate candidates for the title *work of art*. Some may think the very fact that the motorcycles have been exhibited in a museum confers the status of works of art (see Dickie 1969). But plenty of objects are exhibited in museums for their historical value, so a case would have to be made for thinking that their aesthetic value, if they have any, is the reason for the exhibition. And, in any case, this seems to get the explanation the wrong way round: objects are exhibited because they are considered works of art and not considered works of art because they are exhibited. We wouldn't say that had Picasso not exhibited *Guernica* (1937), it would not have been a work of art, nor do we think that just because Paul McCartney or Prince Charles exhibit their paintings that they are works of art.

However, the issue is not as straightforward as this. In a 2004 poll of five hundred British art experts (artists, critics, curators and others), Marcel Duchamp's *Fountain* (1917), which is a urinal with 'R Mutt' (the name of a firm of sanitary engineers) signed on it, was considered, with sixty-four per cent of the vote, the most influential work of the twentieth century, ahead of Picasso's *Les Demoiselles d'Avignon* (1907), with forty-two per cent and Warhol's *Marilyn* (1964), with twenty-nine per cent. *Fountain* would not ordinarily have been considered as art (or even anti-art) had it not been put forward as an object for contemplation in such a setting. Duchamp took the idea that any object can be the object of aesthetic contemplation to its logical conclusion: what are we to say of the 'ready-made' urinal? If we find aesthetic value in an object whose sole function is for men to piss in (and, all too commonly, around), the very notion of a work of art, we would think, must be as empty as Duchamp's bladder. Yet *Fountain* became an icon. *That* is the profound paradox which lies at the heart of much modern art, so arguably *Fountain* does deserve to be voted the most influential 'work' of the twentieth century.

There is, then, a subtle complexity in the relationship between works and their featuring in established institutions of the art world but it is not a relationship we need to get into. It seems to me that the motorcycles which feature in art galleries are not presented as anti-art or as an attempt at post-modern irony. Some may take it to be a statement that any old object can be considered as an object of aesthetic contemplation but if so, Duchamp did it first and better. It is doubtful, then, that this can be the point (although, admittedly, Warhol's *Brillo Boxes* (1964) and Emin's *My Bed* (1999) are later variations on this theme, so why not bikes?). Maybe the point is to advertise, and make less alien, the idea of a museum to the great unwashed who are the biking community via some low-brow objects that are intellectually accessible to them. Or maybe it is just to make some money. Whether or not there is some truth in these suggested motivations, none of them are primary reasons for the exhibitions. I think there is a better answer: unlike Duchamp's bog-standard urinal, bikes naturally lend themselves to being objects of aesthetic evaluation *as we commonly employ the notion* and so it is worth displaying them in this capacity.

What is the problem? Why on earth would you *not* think that motorcycles could be works of art, given that we can truly apply terms such as 'beautiful' to them? Well, people and sunsets are also subject to such evaluation and yet are not works of art. The same can be said of the menacing growl of the typical Ducati four-stroke 90 degree V-twin (or, rather, L-twin) engine, which to my ears is far superior to the harsher, more abrasive sound of the typical Harley-Davidson four-stroke 45 degree V-twin. The reason applying aesthetic terms to these things doesn't show that they are works of art is because they are not *works* at all. (Let's set aside people with a penchant for cosmetic surgery or those environments that only look the way they do because of human intervention, and let's assume that the sounds generated by motorcycle engines are a *mere consequence* of how the engines are constructed and not something which is *intended* – although specifying the difference between intending some desired end, like an engine, but not its known consequences, like its sound, is a notoriously difficult philosophical problem.)

Since motorcycles (whatever we decide about the noise they make) *are* works, can we appeal to the fact that certain terms apply to them, in order to say that they are works of art? Not necessarily: we would have to be sure that in applying the terms, they were being used to evaluate the bike *as a work of art*, rather than as its capacity as something else. What does this attitude of aesthetic appreciation amount to?

BIKERS WITH ATTITUDES

There is a host of theories concerning what it is to have an aesthetic appreciation of an object. Must we take some special attitude towards a bike, such that it counts as seeing it as an aesthetic object as opposed to something else? There is a tradition, of which Immanuel Kant is part, which takes 'disinterest' as the characteristic attitude involved in aesthetic contemplation, where 'disinterest' can roughly be taken to mean we have no interest in the *practical* uses of the object (see Kant 1790).

Is disinterestedness, in this sense, the sort of attitude we take towards evaluating motorcycles? If it isn't, then according to this theory, we can't be evaluating the motorcycle aesthetically. Luckily, we *can* adopt such an attitude towards motorcycles: I did it when searching around for my first bike (a Ducati Monster). I didn't need one for travelling; I wasn't really aware of the sensual pleasures generated by twisting the throttle, leaning into corners or braking heavily at high speed to reach crawling pace in a matter of a few seconds. I just fell in love with the *look* of it; I bought it *primarily on the basis of its styling.* So, not only is the disinterested attitude possible when contemplating bikes; it actually happens. And not just to me: in my experience, a Ducati merely parked in the street can draw a crowd of admirers who will stand and stare for longer than they know they really should. The notion of disinterest also seems to capture, to a certain extent, our aesthetic *experience*, for when we are fully absorbed in an object such as a beautiful bike, we do feel a certain detachment from the world of practical affairs.

It seems to me that it isn't just the appearance of the motorcycle that grounds its aesthetic evaluation. To aesthetically appreciate the object fully, certain contexts of evaluation have to be invoked, such as its history or the means by which it was produced. Although not many people are aware of these contexts in any detail, they are aware of other things available to look at and that there is something extraordinary, relative to the others, about the particular object before them. As David Daiches (1969) argues in the case of literature, to develop an aesthetic appreciation of objects, we need to encounter and engage with a wide range of possibilities: aesthetic appreciation is essentially comparative. We can add that, because there is more, or less, to know about the contexts of evaluation as much as the internal structure of the work itself, aesthetic appreciation also comes by degrees. To me, the Ducati Monster looks so much better than other bikes in the 'urban warrior' style (a comparative context of evaluation) but it emerges as an even more remarkable achievement when we learn that the design is over ten years old, still going strong and initiated an explosion of bikes in this style from other manufacturers (an historical context of evaluation). Nevertheless, even if we add these contexts of evaluation, I think the attitude of disinterest is an inappropriate attitude to take towards bikes, if we require a complete aesthetic appreciation of them. I shall argue for this in the last section.

For the time being, suppose we accept that this sketch of the aesthetic attitude is fundamentally correct. We still have the problem of *taste*. In general, there does not seem to be a special sense by which we perceive aesthetic properties, such as the beauty, elegance or garishness of objects. What we see are various arrangements of the component parts, from which we make aesthetic judgements. It is common for people to disagree in their judgements of the aesthetic properties of an object, which makes some believe that it is an entirely subjective matter. If someone claims that the Honda Gold Wing is an elegant bike, whereas someone else claims it is one of the ugliest contraptions on the road, there is no fact of the matter as to who is correct: 'It's a matter of taste.'

However, more needs to be said, to make this position palatable. I think many of us would be reluctant to call the Gold Wing 'elegant'. We'd be wondering by *which* criteria someone could judge it to be elegant. It is comfortable for long journeys, smooth, useful, allows for good communication between driver and passenger, has a reverse gear, and so on. We'd check that this wasn't what they meant by 'elegant', but if they claimed that it really wasn't and they genuinely thought it was elegant in the disinterested sense sketched above, we'd have to show them other bikes and compare their responses to get a feel for what they meant and to check they really did have a good knowledge of how elegant motorcycles can be. If, after establishing that they meant by 'elegant' what we meant and that they had as much knowledge of motorcycles as we had, we'd have nothing more to say and all we could do would be to get on our respective bikes and continue on our way.

This seems to me to be correct. We are rightly irritated by those who make aesthetic judgements (often very loudly) on things of which they evidently know nothing at all. This sketch of an account accords with this feeling that the philistines are wrong, for it allows us to have genuine disagreement about something and for there to be clear criteria by which we evaluate the merits of the respective positions. It isn't the case that 'anything goes' in aesthetic evaluations: some people are better judges than others (as Hume (1757) points out) but among those who are equally informed and equally considered to be good judges, a respectful acknowledgement of differences seems to be the right approach.

We've arrived at the conclusion that motorcycles can be objects of aesthetic contemplation. Some might think that, since the phrase 'work of art' is nowadays so broad as to be practically empty, this is not of much consequence. Perhaps, but showing that it is legitimate to consider them as works of art is only half the task, since that conclusion alone doesn't show us what sort of art objects they are. *How* they work as art objects is the interesting question.

By far the best way to proceed is to accept that some objects are paradigm cases of works of art: if anything is a work of art, then these things are. We can then use them to discuss what the relevant similarities and differences are between these paradigms and motorcycles, to determine their nature as works of art.

DO MANY MOTORCYCLES ON THE ROAD CREATE MORE ROADWORKS OR MORE ARTWORKS?

What are the paradigmatic art forms that share structural similarities with motorcycles? So far, we have been talking about the aesthetics of motorcycles in terms of their visual appearance so perhaps we should liken them to paintings. If we do, we come across the following problem: according to the philosopher, Richard Wollheim (1980), painting, by its very nature, produces a *unique* item (a certain arrangement of paint on a particular canvas) that we identify as the art object. However, although there are one-off motorcycles, the majority of those we are considering as artworks are mass-produced: there are *many* instances of the Ducati 916. Consider going to the *Louvre* to see the *Mona Lisa*: it is essential to seeing the work of art that we see *that* instance, whereas when people went to the exhibitions at the Guggenheim museums, any old instance of the Ducati 916 would have sufficed for them to appreciate the Ducati 916 – the first one has no more standing than the last. If we were to burn the *Mona Lisa*, the artwork would be destroyed, whereas if we crashed a Ducati 916, we could buy another or borrow a good friend's (so long as we didn't keep doing it ...).

We might respond that the *Mona Lisa could* have had many instances (even though it doesn't). If this were true, it wouldn't matter that there are many instances of certain bikes, so this fact alone would not rule out a comparison between bikes and paintings. The philosopher, Gregory Currie, disagrees with Wollheim that painting produces an essentially unique physical object. According to Currie (1989), a work of art is a *type of action* which produces such objects as paint on canvas. Since the work of art is a *type* of action, it could have been done by any-one, at any time, just as much as *changing some sparkplugs* is a type of action which can be done on many different occasions by many different people. Even though Leonardo da Vinci was the only one to produce the physical object which we call '*Mona Lisa*' in the way that he did, someone else could have acted to produce a qualitatively identical object in the same way and thus produced another instance of that work of art. This might be highly unlikely but that's not to say it couldn't happen.

However, even if we accept that the number of instances of the work does not affect its being likened to painting, there remains a fundamental difference between motorcycles and paintings. There is an intimate relationship between the artist and the instance of the work they produce: *the artists themselves* have to apply the paint for it to be *their* work. This is certainly not the case in the production of a motorcycle: Massimo Tamburini did not have to build each Ducati 916 for us to recognise it as being his work. So painting, even though it is a visual art form, is not the paradigm we're after.

We need not look far for art forms which are similar to bikes, however. Literature and music (and film, if we want a visual element) allow for many instances of works to exist and neither requires that the artist execute each of the instances. Books are instances of the artworks of the authors and we can liken their printers to the spray painters and engineers who put bikes together. In this respect there is only one work of art that is the Ducati 916, just as there is only one novel which is *Nausea*. Both have many instances manufactured by many people, yet we see the works as the remarkable achievements of Tamburini and Jean-Paul Sartre.

This is a nice account, since it accords with our wanting to evaluate the artwork as an achievement of the artist, given the contexts of evaluation mentioned above. What might make philosophers queasy is the status of the artwork in this account: what *is* it? According to this view, it *isn't* each instance. We don't think it is much of an artistic achievement to produce the thousandth Ducati 916. Neither do we think that Sartre's original manuscript for *Nausea* has any more claim to be *the* work of art than the copy on my shelf. (If it did, Sartre's spelling mistakes, handwriting and the original French would have to be present in all instances. This is clearly wrong.) Sartre's manuscript has more historical, sentimental and economic value than my copy and Sartre might have had such remarkable handwriting that the manuscript is itself aesthetically valuable but these considerations are irrelevant to the evaluation of the *content* of the manuscript, that is, the novel. The same goes for the first (as well as the last) instance of the Ducati 916.

What *is* the work of art? Seen as a type of action by an artist, it seems to have become a rather mysterious thing, unlike the tangible instances of it on which we can burn some rubber, pull wheelies and pose. However, since we are quite happy with the notion of a type of action in general, like *changing the spark-plugs*, we can leave this issue unresolved and needn't lose too much sleep over it.

FROM SPARE PART TO *HIGH* ART?

Even if some people were willing to concede that motorcycles can be artworks, many would be unwilling to place them 'up there' with other more conventional art forms. They might say, 'Sure, call it art if you likes but it ain't no *high* art.' Do such, seemingly cultured, people have a real distinction in mind or is it more of a personal agenda (such as keeping others in their place or indicating social or intellectual status)? Part of the controversy over having motorcycles exhibited in art galleries was, no doubt, due to the distinction between 'high' and 'low' art: motorcycles, being of the low variety, have no place in galleries. Often-cited paradigms of high art are classical music, ballet and poetry, whereas rock music, hip-hop dancing and stand-up comedy are low. However, it seems to me the distinction has no real basis, or at least, no useful function. (I'll leave aside the separate, sociological, question of why some people feel the need to draw the distinction.)

Is it a distinction between 'good' and 'bad' art, with high art being good and low art being bad? It can't be. Although there is some sublime classical music, there are also tediously bland works. (Mozart, in my view, is an example of someone who has produced music in both categories.) And some rock music is extraordinarily complex, exciting and original.[1]

The sociologist, Herbert Gans (1974), relates the notions of high and low art to that of high and low culture, which themselves are related to socio-economic position. If this were right, it would be a surprise that a philosopher from Cambridge University could be an avid consumer of rock and jazz music, stand-up comedy and television, classical music and painting but not care much for poetry and theatre. But it isn't.

Some characterise the distinction by saying that low art is mass-produced (at least the instances, or copies of the instances, are), formulaic, accessible, requires only passive reception and is too involved with economic and social pressures to have the autonomy required of works of art. However, these criteria cut across the high-low distinction, as usually characterised in terms of different art forms and genres: I'd bet more people have heard Beethoven's Fifth Symphony than have seen *any* Moto Guzzi motorcycle; much rock and jazz music is not formulaic but in any sense that some of it is (for example, use of 12-bar blues) some classical music is just as subject to the charge (for example in the widespread use of the cycle of fifths in baroque music); the use of classical pieces in television

---

[1] Consider, for instance, the genre known as 'progressive rock', which has fruitfully developed in the hands of bands like *Dream Theater*, or even the slightly more mainstream but thoroughly astonishing guitar work by Brian May on the *Queen* albums of the 70s. Indeed, I would like to see anyone who has this 'low' opinion of electric guitar music to defend the high-low distinction after listening to players such as Al Di Meola, Allan Holdsworth, John McLaughlin, Joe Satriani and Steve Vai, to name but a few of my favourites.

advertisements and the popularity of poster prints of modern paintings indicates that accessibility is likely to be a function of familiarity rather than something intrinsic to painting or classical music; given the ubiquity of such works in popular culture, they are as passively received as any 'low' art (although, it must be said, to appreciate any artwork fully requires active participation at some level and an awareness of its setting within a context) and there have been many composers who have composed work to please their benefactors, whereas there is a substantial network of independent record labels which specialise in promoting pioneering rock and jazz musicians without compromising the integrity of their work.

In a nutshell, it is rather ridiculous to make a distinction between high and low art, if it's supposed to capture some intrinsic difference in quality between art-forms (how can painting be better than comedy?) or within the same art-form but across genres (how can Gregorian chant be better than jazz–rock fusion?). Denying there is any real basis for the distinction is not to say that anything goes: we can still say, as we should want to, that within a given genre, some artworks are better than others. What we can't say is that if motorcycles are works of art, then they are immediately of a lower status than other art-forms. Whether it is a good art piece or not has to be based on its *particular* merits against a context of evaluation, as we've already discussed.

There may still be some nagging doubt that motorcycles cannot count as genuine works of art because we do not yet know how we are supposed to evaluate them as art objects. That's because I have not yet identified the art form to which they are most allied, which is what I'll now do.

There are some, for instance Arthur Danto (1981; 1997), who think that what is characteristic of a work of art is that a message must be put across that requires some kind of interpretation on the part of someone observing the work. In other words, the work has to be *about* something; perhaps the most satisfying art pieces are those that require difficult probing to determine what that thing is. If this is true, then it is odd to consider motorcycles to be works of art, since it is not obvious that they are about *anything*, let alone anything deep.

However, this isn't a particularly strong reason for not taking bikes to be works of art. First, it is not clear that works of art, as we ordinarily understand the notion, need be *about* anything at all. Certainly, the majority of literary works are about something and require some interpretation, but Hugo Ball, a contributor to the early twentieth century *avant-garde* art movement known as 'Dada', produced entirely abstract 'phonetic poetry', some of which begins:

gadji beri bimba
glandridi lauli lonni cadori

This clearly lacks meaning, in the usual sense of the word. At most, we can say that it is about *itself* (in the sense that it is about the sound and rhythm of the words used) but it is not a candidate for any interpretation beyond this. You would, quite naturally, feel the need to discover the meaning behind the action of anyone who performed the poem, given its bizarreness, and there might be some profound point trying to be conveyed in using those words in that way; but this is distinct from what the poem is about.

Dada pieces, however, are considered by many to be more 'anti-art' than art and so may not fit our idea of a paradigmatic case of an artwork, but we need not look far for relatively unproblematic works of art which are not about anything.[2] Paintings often need to be interpreted for us to determine what they mean but Piet Mondrian's famous series of 'neo-plastic' paintings, in which he limits himself to rectangular forms, primary colours and black, white and grey, or the paintings of Mark Rothko, with large rectangular expanses of colour arranged vertically with hazy edges, resulting in a vibrant, pulsating image, show that paradigmatic artworks need not be about anything (other than the artwork itself and perhaps also in reference to other artworks). The fact that an artwork might invoke a particular emotion in the observer does not show that it is *about* that feeling, any more than someone telling you the price of an MV Agusta is *about* the emotions you feel when your dreams are crushed. In any case, anyone who knows anything about music knows it is implausible to think that all music represents or is about something (other than itself and perhaps other pieces of music) and so will wonder what all this fuss concerning abstract art is about anyway.

However, rather than say that, to be works of art, bikes are not about anything and need not be about anything, I'd rather say that bikes *are* about something; for one thing, they are about *bikes*. Just as some music is about the arrangement of sounds and some painting is about the arrangement

---

[2] For more on Dada, see Richter (1964).

of shapes and colours, bikes are about the arrangement of bike parts.

There are, however, two seeming disanalogies. First, *some* music and *some* painting *is* about something external, whereas *no* bikes are. Second, bikes cannot be arranged any old way but there are no such constraints on music and painting. There are certain constraints to which one must conform if the work is to be recognised as falling within a particular style or form but the artist has a choice over which constraints, if any, they impose on themselves, which is not the case when conceiving of a motorcycle.

The first objection is easily dealt with, since it is not essential that a motorcycle not make reference to something outside itself (and other motorcycles). As will be well-known to any-one who has seen *American Chopper*, Orange County Choppers have famously produced motorcycles representing an American fire engine, a Comanche helicopter (see image 6), the Statue of Liberty and even Christmas by, among other things, shaping the handlebars to resemble reindeer antlers. There is nothing *in principle* that stops motorcycles from representing something else (in these cases by straightforwardly resembling those things) and so, no intrinsic difference between what motorcycles can do in this regard and what other art forms can.

What about the fact that bikes cannot be arranged any old how, in the way music and painting can? Motorcycles have a function which seems to distinguish them from other paradigmatic works of art: they are primarily designed to get the rider from A to B, which does not seem to give rise to any aesthetic evaluation at all; indeed, any aesthetic evaluation seems to be of secondary importance, which is odd for a work of art.

For this reason, rather than drawing the conclusion that motorcycles are not genuine works of art, I take this to give us an insight into how we should treat them as works of art. The consideration of utility is what distinguishes at least one art-form from the others: architecture differs from sculpture in just this way. In architecture, utility plays at least some part in the aesthetic evaluation of the piece. So the position that I have arrived at is: if architecture is considered a branch of the arts, then motorcycles should be evaluated along similar lines to architecture.

This is precisely why I said that the attitude of disinterest is entirely inappropriate when contemplating motorcycles as works of art. *Styling*, which solely concerns appearance, together with the historical and comparative contexts of evaluation, is not all that is relevant when evaluating a bike aesthetically. *Design*, which concerns problem-solving, is also crucial. But what are we looking for, such that we can say not just that these things work well but that they are works of art; and have some profound import, of the sort we want from great works of art? Well, I think that Charlotte and Peter Fiell (2001: 5) put it superbly:

Design is not only a process linked to mechanised production, it is a means of conveying persuasive ideas, attitudes and values about how things could or should be according to individual, corporate, institutional or national objectives. As a channel of communication between people, design provides a particular insight into the character and thinking of the designer and his/her beliefs about what is important in the relationship between the object (design solution), the user/consumer and the design process and society.

To expand the point, consider the influential German *Bauhaus* school of architecture and design, which flourished during the 1920s. The principles they adopted as constituting good design emphasised a strict economy of means and the use of the ideal materials for the job. This resulted in a severe, impersonal but clean and refined geometrical style.

Famously, Ludwig Mies van der Ruhe designed the Seagram Building in Manhattan (1954–1958) along Bauhaus principles.[3] To promote the Bauhaus philosophy, it was important that the building expressed the way it was constructed. Although he chose not to show the diagonal steel bracings that stop the building collapsing sideways, he did want to show the main steel columns. The problem was that these needed to be encased in concrete to make them more fire-resistant. So Mies van der Ruhe decided to encase these now concrete-coated steel beams in a top coat of steel, to show that steel beams had been used in the initial construction of the building! But should he have left the concrete exposed, since, arguably, it was just as much required in the building's construction? It looks like he did not have a solution which could satisfy all his requirements: either he couldn't show what he took to be the important part of the construction or he couldn't avoid using superfluous steel, thereby violating the Bauhaus principles.

Contrast this with the minimalist design of the Ducati 916 and the less minimalist Harley V-Rod. Both these motorcycles express their own construction – but *authentically*! For me, this is the feature that makes the V-Rod so much more attractive than the Harleys that have gone before it. They tend to hide

---

[3] See, for example, Ballantyne (2002).

the frame to accentuate the engine and bodywork, whereas the V-Rod celebrates its chassis. Unlike the Seagram building there are no artificial means used to express the construction of either motorcycle: the design takes care of that. Suppose we adopted the Bauhaus principles of design as a statement of our vision of how things should be. We would then have clear criteria by which we could judge a particular motorcycle as a solution to the motorcycle design problem. At this point, the V-Rod starts to struggle, for the severe lack of ground clearance when cornering shows that its styling has compromised its functionality, whereas, with the Ducati, styling and functionality go hand in hand, satisfying the Bauhaus requirements well. Of course, we might reject the Bauhaus principles, but adopting such a framework would allow the Ducati to count not just as a great motorcycle but as a great work of art.[4]

[4] A version of this chapter was first published as Bourne (2006b).

REFERENCES

AASHTO. 1994. 'The National Statutory Speed Limit', American Association of State Highway Transportation Officials, Policy Resolution PR-5–93.

Armstrong, D. M. 1968. *A Materialist Theory of the Mind*. London, Routledge.

Ashton, S. J. and Mackay, G. M. 1979. 'Some characteristics of the population who suffer trauma as pedestrians when hit by cars and some resulting implications', 4th IRCOBI International Conference, Göthenborg.

Ballantyne, A. 2002. *Architecture*. Oxford, Oxford University Press.

Bentham, J. 1789. *Introduction to the Principles of Morals and Legislation*, J. H. Burns and H. L. A. Hart (eds.) Oxford, Oxford University Press, 1982.

Bourne, C. P. 2006a. *A Future for Presentism*. Oxford, Oxford University Press.

—— 2006b. 'From Spare Part to High Art: the Aesthetics of Motorcycles', in B. E. Rollin, *et al.* (eds.) *Harley-Davidson and Philosophy*. Chicago, Open Court, 2006, 101–16.

Burgess, A. 1962. *A Clockwork Orange*. London, Penguin.

Burnet, J. 1892. *Early Greek Philosophy*. London, A and C Black.

Camus, A. 1942. *The Myth of Sisyphus*, trans. J. O'Brien. London, Penguin, 1955.

Carruthers, P. 1992. *The Animals Issue: Moral Theory in Practice.* Cambridge, Cambridge University Press.

Cottingham, J. 1978. 'A Brute to the Brutes? Descartes' Treatment of Animals', *Philosophy*, 53, 551–9.

Cottingham, J., Stoothoff, R., Murdoch, D. and Kenny, A. (eds.) 1991. *The Philosophical Writings of Descartes*, Volume III, *The Correspondence*. Cambridge, Cambridge University Press.

Currie, G. 1989. *An Ontology of Art*. London, Macmillan.

Daiches, D. 1969. 'Literary Evaluation', in J. P. Strelka (ed.), *Problems of Literary Evaluation*, Yearbook of Comparative Criticism, Volume 2. University Park, Pennsylvania State University Press.

Dancy, J. 1985. *Introduction to Contemporary Epistemology*. Oxford, Blackwell.

Danto, A. 1981. *Transfiguration of the Commonplace*. Cambridge, Mass., Harvard University Press.

—— 1997. *After the End of Art*. Princeton, Princeton University Press.

Davidson, D. 1975. 'Thought and Talk', in his *Inquiries into Truth and Interpretation*. Oxford, Oxford University Press, 155–70.

Dennett, D. 1971. 'Intentional Systems', *Journal of Philosophy*, 68, 87–106, which also appears in his *Brainstorms*. Penguin, 1978, 3–22.

—— 1987. *The Intentional Stance*. Cambridge, MA., Bradford Books/The MIT Press.

—— 1995. 'Animal Consciousness', *Social Research*, 62, 691–710.

Descartes, R. 1637. *Discourse on the Method of Properly Conducting One's Reason and of Seeking the Truth in the Sciences*, readily available in the Penguin edition *Discourse of Method and the Meditations*, trans. F. E. Sutcliffe. London, Penguin, 1968.

—— 1641. *Meditations on the First Philosophy in which the Existence of God and the Real Distinction between the Soul and the Body of Man are Demonstrated*, readily available in the Penguin edition *Discourse of Method and the Meditations*, trans. F. E. Sutcliffe. London, Penguin, 1968.

References

Devlin, P. 1965. *The Enforcement of Morals*. Oxford, Oxford University Press.

Dickie, G. 1969. 'Defining Art', *American Philosophical Quarterly*, 6, 253–56.

Elliot, R. 1982. 'Faking Nature', *Inquiry*, 25, 81–93.

—— 1995. 'Introduction', in R. Elliot (ed.), *Environmental Ethics*. Oxford, Oxford University Press, 1995, 1–20.

Epicurus, *Letter to Menoeceus*, trans. Cyril Bailey from *Epicurus: The Extant Remains*, trans. Cyril Bailey. Oxford, Oxford University Press, 1926.

Feldman, F. 2006. 'Harleys as Freedom Machines: Myth or Fantasy?', in B. E. Rollin, *et al.* (eds.) *Harley-Davidson and Philosophy*. Chicago, Open Court, 89–99.

Ferriss, S. 2006. 'Leather-Clad: Eroticism, Fetishism and Other -isms in Biker Fashion' in B. E. Rollin, *et al.* (eds.) *Harley-Davidson and Philosophy*. Chicago, Open Court, 157–66.

Fiell, C. and P. 2001. *Design of the 20th Century*. Cologne, Taschen.

Freud, S. 1920. *Beyond the Pleasure Principle*, in J. Strachey (ed.) *The Standard Edition of the Complete Psychological Works of Sigmund Freud*. London, 1953–74, vol.18, 7–64.

—— 1930. *Civilisation and its Discontents*, in J. Strachey (ed.) *The Standard Edition of the Complete Psychological Works of Sigmund Freud*. London, 1953–74, vol. 21, 59–145.

—— 1938. *An Outline of Psycho-Analysis*, in J. Strachey (ed.) *The Standard Edition of the Complete Psychological Works of Sigmund Freud*. London, 1953–74, vol.23, 141–207.

Gans, H. 1974. *Popular Culture and High Culture*. New York, Basic Books.

Goodall, J. 1971. *In the Shadow of Man*. Boston, Houghton Mifflin.

Hart, H. L. A. 1963. *Law, Liberty, Morality*. Oxford, Oxford University Press.

—— 1968. *Punishment and Responsibility*. Oxford, Clarendon Press.

Heidegger, M. 1927. *Being and Time*, trans. J. Macquarrie and E. Robinson. Oxford. Blackwell, 1962.

Hume, D. 1748. *An Enquiry concerning Human Understanding*, first published as *Philosophical Essays concerning Human Understanding*. London; repr., L. A. Selby-Bigge and P. H. Nidditch (eds.) *Enquiries Concerning Human Understanding and Concerning the Principles of Morals*. Oxford, Clarendon Press, 1978.

—— 1751. *An Enquiry Concerning the Principles of Morals*. London; repr., ed. L. A. Selby-Bigge and P. H. Nidditch (eds.) *Enquiries Concerning Human Understanding and Concerning the Principles of Morals*. Oxford, Clarendon Press, 1978.

—— 1757. 'Of the Standard of Taste', in S. Feagin and P. Maynard (eds.), *Aesthetics*. Oxford, Oxford University Press, 1997, 350–64.

Husserl, E. 1900–1. *Logical Investigations*, trans. J. N. Findlay. London, Routledge, 1900/01; 2nd, revised edition. London, Routledge, 1913.

Joksch, H. C. 1993. 'Velocity change and fatality risk in a crash – a rule of thumb', *Accident, Analysis and Prevention*, 25, 103–4.

Kant, I. *Lectures on Ethics*, trans. L. Infield. New York, Harper Torchbooks, 1963.

—— 1790. *Critique of Judgement*. Oxford, Clarendon Press, 1952.

Kieffner, G. L. 2006. 'The Wild One, She-Devils on Wheels and "Motorcycle Syndrome": Foucault and Biker Images', in B. E. Rollin, *et al.* (eds.) *Harley-Davidson and Philosophy*. Chicago, Open Court, 167–81.

Krens, T. *et al.* 2001. *The Art of the Motorcycle*. New York, Guggenheim Museum Publications.

Kripke, S. A. 1980. *Naming and Necessity*. Oxford, Blackwell.

Lewis, D. 1976. 'Survival and Identity', in A. O. Rorty (ed.) *The Identities of Persons*. University of California Press, 1976, 17–40; also in his *Philosophical Papers*, Volume I. Oxford, Oxford University Press, 1986, 55–77.

—— 1980. 'Mad Pain and Martian Pain', in Ned Block (ed.), *Readings in the Philosophy of Psychology*, Volume I. Harvard University Press, 1980, 216–22; also in his *Philosophical Papers*, Volume I. Oxford, Oxford University Press, 1986, 122–32.

—— 1996. 'Illusory innocence?', *Eureka Street*, 5, 35–6; also in his *Papers in Ethics and Social Philosophy*. Cambridge, Cambridge University Press, 2000, 152–8.

—— 1997. 'Do we believe in penal substitution?', *Philosophical Papers*, 26, 203–9; also in his *Papers in Ethics and Social Philosophy*. Cambridge, Cambridge University Press, 2000, 128–35.

Lieber, J. 1988. 'Cartesian Linguistics?' *Philosophia*, 118, 309–46.

Lucretius, *De Rerum Natura*, trans. John Dryden, in D. J. Enright (ed.) *The Oxford Book of Death*. Oxford, Oxford University Press.

Mackie, J. L. 1977. *Ethics: Inventing Right and Wrong*. London, Penguin.

Mellor, D. H. 1980. 'Consciousness and Degrees of Belief' in his *Matters of Metaphysics*. Cambridge, Cambridge University Press, 1991, 30–60.

—— 2005. *Probability: A Philosophical Introduction*. London, Routledge.

Mill, J. S. 1859. *On Liberty*, in J. M. Robson (ed.), *Collected Works of John Stuart Mill*, Volume 18. London, Routledge, 1991, 213–310.

—— 1861. *Utilitarianism*, in J. M. Robson (ed.), *Collected Works of John Stuart Mill*, Volume 10. London, Routledge, 1991, 203–59.

Mustienes, C. and Hilland, T. (eds.) 2006. *Signs*. Cologne, Taschen.

Nagel, T. 1970. 'Death', in his *Mortal Questions*. Cambridge, Cambridge University Press, 1979, 1–10.

—— 1971. 'The Absurd', in his *Mortal Questions*. Cambridge, Cambridge University Press, 1979, 11–23.

Nietzsche, F. 1906. *The Will to Power*, posthumous notes from 1883–8 trans. W. Kaufmann. New York, Viking, 1967.

Nozick, R. 1974. *Anarchy, State and Utopia*. Oxford, Blackwell.

—— 1997. 'On the Randian Argument', in his *Socratic Puzzles*. Cambridge, Mass., Harvard University Press, 249–64.

Parfit, D. 1984. *Reasons and Persons*. Oxford, Oxford University Press.

Pirsig, R. M. 1974. *Zen and the Art of Motorcycle Maintenance*. New York, William Morrow & Company, Inc.

Polhemus, T. 2001. 'The Art of the Motorcycle: Outlaws, Animals and Sex Machines', in T. Krens, *et al., The Art of the Motorcycle*. New York, Guggenheim Museum Publications, 2001, 48–59.

Priest, G. 2006. 'Zen and the Art of Harley Riding', in B. E. Rollin, *et al.* (eds.) *Harley-Davidson and Philosophy*. Chicago, Open Court, 2006, 3–10.

Putnam, H. 1981. *Reason, Truth and History*. Cambridge, Cambridge University Press.

Rawls, J. 1971. *A Theory of Justice*. Oxford, Oxford University Press.

Richter, H. 1964. *Dada: Art and Anti-Art*. London, Thames and Hudson.

Sartre, J-P. 1938. *Nausea*, trans. R. Baldick. London, Penguin.

—— 1945a. *The Age of Reason*, trans. E. Sutton. London, Penguin.

—— 1945b. *The Reprieve*, trans. E. Sutton. London, Penguin.

—— 1958. *Being and Nothingness: An Essay on Phenomenological Ontology*, trans. H. E. Barnes. London, Methuen & Co. Ltd; first published as *L'Etre et le Néant*. Gallimard, 1943.

Sato, I. 2001. 'Bosozoku (motorcycle gangs)', in T. Krens, *et al., The Art of the Motorcycle*. New York, Guggenheim Museum Publications, 2001, 82–9.

Simon, A. 2001. 'Freedom or Death: Notes on the Motorcycle in Film and Video', in T. Krens, *et al., The Art of the Motorcycle*. New York, Guggenheim Museum Publications, 2001.

Singer, P. 1975. *Animal Liberation*, 2nd edition. New York, New York Review/Random House, 1990.

—— 1995. *Rethinking Life and Death: The Collapse of Our Traditional Ethics*. Oxford, Oxford University Press.

Sober, E. 1986. 'Philosophical Problems for Environmentalism', in B. Norton (ed.), *The Preservation of Species: the Value of Biological Diversity*. Princeton, Princeton University Press, 1986, 173–95.

Sorabji, R. 1993. *Animal minds & human morals: the origins of the Western debate*. London, Duckworth.

References

Stephen, J. F. 1873. *Liberty, Equality, Fraternity*. Chicago, IL, University of Chicago Press, 1991.

Stoppard, T. 1967. *Rosencrantz and Guildenstern Are Dead*. London, Faber and Faber.

Unger, P. 1995. *Living High and Letting Die: Our Illusion of Innocence*. Oxford, Oxford University Press.

Williams, B. 1973. 'The Makropulos case; reflections on the tedium of immortality', in his *Problems of the Self*. Cambridge, Cambridge University Press, 82–100.

Wittgenstein, L. 1921. *Tractatus Logico-Philosophicus*, trans. C. K. Ogden. London, Routledge.

Wolfenden, J. (chair). 1957. 'The Report of the Committee on Homosexual Offences and Prostitution' (cmnd 247), HMSO.

Wollheim, R. 1980. *Art and its Objects*. Cambridge, Cambridge University Press.

Yourgrau, P. 1987. 'The Dead', *Journal of Philosophy*, 86, 84–101.

INDEX

Index